Science of Coaching

VOLLEYBALL

Science of Coaching Series

DI

Carl McGown, PhD

**Head Volleyball Coach
and Professor of Physical Education
Brigham Young University**

Editor

Human Kinetics Publishers

Library of Congress Cataloging-in-Publication Data

Science of coaching volleyball/Carl McGown, editor
    p. cm.--(Science of coaching series)
    ISBN 0-87322-572-4
    1. Volleyball--Coaching.   I. McGown, Carl, 1937-   II. Series.
  GV1015.5.C63S35 1994
  796.325--dc20   93-24319
                                                    CIP

ISBN: 0-87322-572-4

Acquisitions Editor: Linda Anne Bump, PhD; **Developmental Editors**: June Decker, Lori Garrett, and Patricia Sammann; **Assistant Editors**: Dawn Roselund, Valerie Hall, Ed Giles, and John Wentworth; **Copyeditor**: Jane Bowers; **Proofreader**: Pam Johnson; **Indexer**: Barbara E. Cohen; **Production Director**: Ernie Noa; **Typesetter and Text Layout**: Yvonne Winsor, Julie Overholt, and Denise Lowry; **Text Design**: Keith Blomberg; **Cover Design**: Jack Davis; **Cover Photo**: Dave Black; **Illustrations**: Tim Offenstein; **Interior Photos**: pages 1, 23, 47, 81 courtesy of Mark Philbrick, Brigham Young University; page 99 by Mary Johnson, *The Daily Illini*; page 131 courtesy of L. Budd Thalman, The Pennsylvania State University; **Mac Art**: Studio 2D; **Printer**: Versa Press, Inc.

Human Kinetics books are available at special discounts for bulk purchase. Special editions or book excerpts can also be created to specification. For details, contact the Special Sales Manager at Human Kinetics.

Printed in the United States of America

10 9 8 7 6 5 4 3 2 1

Human Kinetics Publishers
Box 5076, Champaign, IL 61825-5076
1-800-747-4457

Canada: Human Kinetics Publishers, Box 24040, Windsor, ON N8Y 4Y9
1-800-465-7301 (in Canada only)

Europe: Human Kinetics Publishers (Europe) Ltd., P.O. Box IW14,
Leeds LS16 6TR, England
0532-781708

Australia: Human Kinetics Publishers, P.O. Box 80, Kingswood 5062,
South Australia
618-374-0433

New Zealand: Human Kinetics Publishers, P.O. Box 105-231, Auckland 1
(09) 309-2259

Contents

Preface

For millions of athletes around the world, an Olympic medal is the ultimate athletic prize. And since the 1984 Olympics the United States has won more Olympic volleyball medals than any other country. Its men's teams have won three Olympic medals (two gold and a bronze) and its women's teams two (a silver and a bronze).

How have U.S. volleyball teams been able to achieve so much? Of course the marvelous athletes have had a lot to do with it. But two other contributing factors have been the tactics the U.S. coaches teach their players and the teaching methods they employ. *Science of Coaching Volleyball* shares with you play strategies and instructional approaches based on the same principles that guided Doug Beal, Arie Selinger, Marv Dunphy, Terry Liskevich, and Fred Sturm as they coached teams at the highest level of competition.

This book, like the other books in the Science of Coaching series, presents information from six sport sciences—motor learning, psychology, biomechanics, physiology, sports medicine, and nutrition—and translates this information into practical applications for high school and college volleyball coaches. Each chapter is written by an expert both in a subdiscipline of sport science and in volleyball. All chapters begin with a short anecdote before progressing to brief descriptions of basic concepts in that area and then continuing with applications of those ideas to training and technique. As you finish each chapter, you'll not only know what the most current research in that area has shown but also how to apply that information to improving your coaching.

The lead chapter, written by the editor, highlights how to best teach new motor skills and most effectively practice those skills. This chapter explains how to improve player responses and give helpful feedback to players on their performance. Guidelines are provided for designing effective practice sessions that promote skill acquisition.

The second chapter, on sport psychology, focuses on two areas of concern for volleyball coaches: helping players achieve consistent, high-quality performance and coaching effectively during both practice and matches. Developing good performance entails teaching players psychological and interpersonal skills such as mental preparation, self-teaching and correction, stress reduction, confidence building, and team leadership and communication. You'll learn how to create a positive learning environment, give feedback and praise, communicate instructions clearly, and set rules and goals.

The biomechanics chapter gives insight into the optimum body placement and movement for performing volleyball skills. Using extensive illustrations, the authors analyze blocking, spiking, serving, floor defense, and footwork and describe the most efficient and effective techniques. If a skill can be executed in different ways, they indicate which way they believe is the best.

Chapter 4 brings the principles of physiology to the volleyball court and weight room. It explains how physiological concepts, such as the stress-adaptation principle and specificity of training, should be incorporated into volleyball players' strength, vertical jump, endurance, and flexibility training. The chapter also describes how to integrate physiological training into volleyball training, including the use of proper drill formats.

As every coach is concerned about player injury, the chapter on sports medicine addresses both injury prevention and injury recognition and treatment. The authors identify and describe 13 common injuries in volleyball and suggest methods of treatment and rehabilitation.

The final chapter underscores how good nutrition enhances volleyball performance. After identifying the keys to good nutrition and what a healthy diet should contain, the author of this chapter turns to coaching concerns such as how much players should weigh and what they should eat before, during, and after a match. The chapter includes sample menus and tells how to make healthy food available for players; a lesson format for teaching players about good nutrition is also provided.

Only a few of you will have the opportunity to coach at the top level in our sport, but all of you can use the volleyball coaching tactics and methods described here to elevate your team's level of play. By following the suggestions of the knowledgeable authors in this book, you can help your players reach their potential and make coaching more enjoyable for you.

Carl McGown
Brigham Young University

CHAPTER 1

Motor Learning: How to Teach Skills

Carl McGown
Brigham Young University

Shortly before the gold-medal volleyball match of the 1988 Summer Olympics, I was assisting with a USA men's team practice when a Canadian sports broadcaster stopped by, interested in discussing the various practice methods he had been observing. He said the practice methods for the USA men's team were unlike those of any of their competitors. I replied that it was probably because we had Karch Kiraly, Steve Timmons, Craig Buck, and all our other great players. But I knew that our team was also different because the coaches knew and used the principles of motor learning. Ever since

Doug Beal and Bill Neville led the team to preeminence in the early 1980s, the USA men's coaches have used these principles to help develop practice plans. Perhaps your team can benefit from them as well.

When you prepare lessons or practices, you should have some rationale for choosing the methods you select. Can you answer questions like, Why did you teach the skill the way you did? Why did you use that sequence? Why did you use those drills, instructional aids, and cues? Most coaches give answers like, That was the way I was taught, or I saw that drill at the last coaching clinic I attended, or Japan does it. Some even admit, I don't know, it just seemed like a good idea. Such answers are not very compelling to me, because I think teaching is much more than copying others. Teaching is in part a science.

John Wooden, the legendary former UCLA basketball coach, said this about the role of teaching in coaching ("Coaching wisdom," 1988):

> When I was coaching I always considered myself a teacher. Teachers tend to follow the laws of learning better than coaches who don't have any teaching background. A coach is nothing more than a teacher. I used to encourage anyone who wanted to coach to get a degree in teaching so they could apply those principles to athletics. (p. 4)

There are laws or principles of learning that you can use to answer questions like the ones raised. The principles are those of the scientific field called motor learning, an area of psychology that studies factors that influence the learning of motor skills. Research has shown that coaching effectiveness improves when coaches use motor learning principles.

WHY MOTOR LEARNING IS IMPORTANT

Almost everything that a coach does in a practice should be influenced by the principles of motor learning. Suppose you want to teach spiking to your athletes. One of your first decisions must be how you will introduce the new concepts. Should you demonstrate the skill or not? If so, what should be the nature of the demonstration? How short or long should it be? Should you talk along with the demonstration? What should you say, and how much? Motor learning scholars have studied all of these factors and provide excellent guidelines.

Perhaps later in the season the problem is serve reception, and you are looking for a new drill or two to help your team improve. Would some "pepper"—having two players hit the ball back and forth to each other, taking turns setting, spiking, and digging—help? How about spending time passing some balls that are thrown directly to your passers? Should you lump all of your passing time into one block, or would it be better to spend several smaller sessions working on the skill? Once again, motor learning research has found answers to these questions.

Finally, consider a middle blocker who is having trouble blocking the high-outside set. Some feedback from you would probably help. But what kind of feedback, and how often should you give it? Information feedback has been one of the most widely studied areas of motor learning, and there are some very specific guidelines to follow if you want to enhance your ability to provide information to your players.

MOTOR LEARNING CONCERNS IN VOLLEYBALL

The important events in learning a motor skill are contained in a model developed by Gentile (1972), modified by Nixon and Locke (1973), and further modified here to integrate motor learning and volleyball (see Figure 1.1).

According to this model, the student or athlete

1. determines the general goal of the task to be learned,
2. formulates a plan (or motor program) to use on the first attempt,
3. makes the response,
4. attends to feedback,
5. decides how to try to do it next time, and
6. repeats the process.

A parallel part of the model contains a sequence of teacher decisions and potential coaching interventions. Research, which provides the basis for the principles of learning, is also reflected in the model. Figure 1.1 links the athlete, the coach, and research findings; it can also serve as a sort of table of contents for this section of the chapter. Because most of the important coaching tasks are contained in the first four stages, I will

Important events in motor learning
Athlete's sequence

	Identifies relevant stimuli; selects goal	Formulates motor program	Responds	Processes feedback	Decides on changes for next response	Responds again
Coach	Stage 1 Goal presentation	Stage 2 Motor program development	Stage 3 Improving responses	Stage 4 Give information feedback	Stage 5 Assist with the decision	Stage 6 Repeat previous steps
Research	Information processing Demonstration Keys Teaching method	Specificity or generality Transfer Whole versus part practice State-dependent remembering Blocked or random practice Progressions Drills Testing	Massed versus distributed practice Physical fatigue Mental practice	Information feedback Goals for drills Competition Opportunity to respond	Emphasis on goal stage and feedback stage	Utilize all previous concepts

Coach's sequence
Important decisions to facilitate motor learning

Figure 1.1 Critical events in an athlete's learning and parallel coaching responsibilities.
Note. From ''Research on Teaching Physical Education'' by J. Nixon and L. Locke. In *Second Handbook of Research on Teaching* (p. 1213) by R. Travers (Ed.), 1973, Chicago: Rand McNally. Copyright 1973 by American Educational Research Association.

4

focus on those in this section. Thus, the motor learning concerns for a volleyball coach are these:

- Goal presentation (helping players understand how the skills of the game are performed)
- Motor program development (planning practices so the skills of the game are practiced effectively)
- Improving responses
- Giving information feedback to players about their performance

How Can I Help My Players Understand How to Perform the Skills of the Game?

Coaches can help players understand how to perform the skills of the game by limiting the information they give, demonstrating, using keys, and employing a teaching method that facilitates learning.

Limiting the Information Given to Volleyball Players

A primary concept of motor learning is that learners have a finite ability to process information. Coaches can facilitate learning by minimizing the amount of information they present when they are introducing a goal. If you present lots of details all at once, your athletes will simply not remember most of them.

Many volleyball coaches talk too much. They know much about the sport, and they want to share all their knowledge with their athletes. (Other coaches may not know so much, but they still like to talk.) Remember, when you are talking to athletes, they may be getting more information than they can handle, and they are also not practicing. To make certain you don't talk too much or give athletes too much information to process when you are presenting goals, employ these two strategies: demonstrations and keys.

Demonstrations

Motor learning studies have found that the memory retains movement information in the form of an image. Therefore, it makes sense to introduce such information in the form of an image by demonstrating the movement. Other work has shown that people learn most tasks faster when they are shown repeated demonstrations. Gallwey (1974), in his fascinating book *The Inner Game of Tennis*, wrote; "I was beginning to learn what all good [teachers] must learn: that images are better than words, showing better than telling, and too much instruction worse than none" (p. 19).

Keys

Demonstrations alone are not enough. Reseachers have discovered that learners attend to task-irrelevant information when their attention is not directed. Coaches can help overcome this problem and improve learning by using performance cues called keys. Keys are short, concise instructions that serve at least four important functions. They

- condense or chunk information,
- reduce words, thus reducing information processing requirements,
- encourage athletes to attend to important elements of the skill, and
- enhance memory.

An important part of coaching is deciding which keys to use to teach skills and the order in which to present them. (Some evidence suggests that successful teachers do this better than less successful teachers.) Combining the demonstrations and the keys into an effective teaching method is also important.

A Teaching Method

Coaches who realize that athletes have a finite ability to process information want to present the right amount of information at the right speed. Because words mean little to beginners, coaches should avoid constant talk and should keep learners active. (Several studies have found that in a typical class students spend only one third of the time or less on task.) Remember, athletes learn best by seeing and doing. You can get your athletes seeing and doing by including the following steps in your goal presentation method (if the coach already knows the abilities of the athletes, the first two steps can be omitted):

1. Demonstrate the skill.
2. Let the athletes attempt the skill so you can assess their abilities and determine what keys need to be given.
3. Demonstrate the skill, focusing attention on a key.
4. Let the athletes practice, and give them feedback about the key.
5. Demonstrate the skill, focusing attention on the next key.
6. Let the athletes practice again, and give them feedback on the new key.
7. Repeat the process until all keys have been covered.

It is difficult for coaches to know how to choose keys, present them in the proper order, and give the right amount of information at the right speed. At conventions when I talk with coaches about these matters, there is always heated discussion. We usually agree on the concepts, but we seldom agree on the keys or the order in which to present them. I do know that the selection and ordering of keys are important to coaching success. When I teach forearm passing to beginners, I have four keys that I want them to learn, and they come in this order:

- Place wrists and hands together.
- Hit the ball on the forearms.
- Keep the elbows straight.
- Face the ball, angle the arms.

Most skills can be taught with four keys or less. Continue to work on each successive key until the athletes have achieved some success with it.

A beautiful example of the method can be found in an article about teaching a child to fish by Engerbretson (1979) (I have paraphrased a little to make his ideas apply to volleyball):

Remember, too, that children learn best by imitation; that is, by watching and doing, rather than by long, involved, technical explanations. A discussion of horizontal momentum, optimum jumping angles, force conversion, and so on could as well be given in a foreign language for all the good it will do most spikers. The majority of instructors talk too much. *Show* them what to do. Even the simplest jump is made up of many components, and it is usually a mistake to try to emphasize all of these at one time. A beginner cannot mentally concentrate upon timing, the footwork, the jump, the arm swing, ball placement, the contact, and the recovery simultaneously. Therefore, after the child has been given a general introduction to spiking, it is best to concentrate on only one component at a time. For example, have the child do a complete spike, but concentrate only on the footwork at the end of the approach. Don't worry if the rest of the spike isn't exactly right—just emphasize the last two steps. Then, as that particular component becomes a fixed habit, start to concentrate on another aspect of the spike. . . . The rule, then, is let one thing become a habit before moving on to the next. (p. 25)

How Can I Plan Effective Practices?

In the model presented in Figure 1.1, the learner must formulate a motor program. Many motor learning experts believe that the motor program is a type of central representation (an image in the mind) that controls movements. So the movements of volleyball players (serving, passing, spiking, etc.) are controlled by their motor programs. Making certain that athletes develop effective motor programs is a primary task facing coaches.

One way that the USA men's team is unique is the manner in which they develop motor programs. Because their method is different, I will explain, in some depth, the concepts that support what they do. These concepts are based on the issues of specificity versus generality, transfer, whole versus part practice, state-dependent remembering, and random versus blocked practice.

Does General Athletic Ability Really Exist?

Most people believe in general athletic ability. They believe that someone who can play baseball well should be able to play golf well, that someone who can play basketball well should also be able to play volleyball well, and so on. Back in the 1920s and 1930s, several prominent physical educators even developed a number of general athletic ability tests. But modern physical educators, led by a scientist named Franklin Henry, no longer accept the notion of general athletic ability. Instead they believe that abilities are specific to the task or activity. This statement by Henry (1958), even though it was written more than 30 years ago, is typical of the current beliefs: "It is no longer possible to justify the concept of unitary abilities such as coordination and agility since the evidence shows that these abilities are specific to the task or activity" (p. 126).

How Much Will Practice Transfer to a Game Situation?

If motor programs are specific, several predictions follow, such as the prediction that there will not be much motor transfer from task to task. For example, playing pepper might not help a player much with backcourt defense. The issue of transfer is crucial to coaches, who expect every drill players perform and every practice a coach designs to transfer successfully to game situations. But if playing pepper does not improve the skill of digging hard-driven spikes much, it may be because there is not enough transfer between the drill and the competitive activity. The research here is very clear: There is not as much motor transfer as we might think. Schmidt (1975) summarizes the research: "There has been a great deal of research conducted concerning transfer from one variation of a task to another variation of the same task. . . . One is forced to the conclusion that the amount of motor transfer is quite small" (p. 63). The prediction of little transfer is upheld. What prediction could be made about whole versus part practice?

Should My Players Practice All of a Skill or Only Part of a Skill?

This question is complex because there are problems in defining what is a whole and what is a part. In spiking, the whole is the approach, the jump, the arm swing or contact of the ball, and the recovery. A part might be just the approach or the arm swing. If motor programs are specific, and if there is not much transfer between tasks, then when we are helping players develop a motor program, whole practice should be better than part practice. Nixon and Locke (1973) reviewed the research in this area and found that "in the 30 whole-part studies reviewed, not one favored teaching methods that used the part or progressive part methods of instruction. In the majority of studies, some variation of the whole method was associated with superior learning" (p. 1216). Some coaches teach spiking by breaking it into parts. First they work on the spiking action or arm swing against a wall, then they work on the approach without a ball, and finally they combine the two. According to Nixon and Locke, it would be better to start with the whole spike and, as I have recommended, use keys to teach the arm swing and the approach.

How Do Athletes Remember?

Cognitive psychologists have found that remembering is state-dependent, which means that when a person learns something, information about the mood of the learner and the environment is stored in memory with the information learned. Performance is significantly better when the environment in which performance occurs matches the emotional state and the environment in which learning occurs. It's no wonder that an inexperienced athlete has difficulty performing before a large audience, or that there is a home court advantage.

Should Practice Be Blocked or Random?

In other words, should there be variability in practice? Armed with the knowledge of specificity, little transfer, the superiority of whole practice, and the state-dependency of learning and remembering, let's make one last prediction: Drills that introduce the variability normally found in a game (random practice) will transfer better to game conditions than drills in which the trials are blocked. For instance, in a blocked practice of the forearm pass, the ball comes from the same place to the same place, allowing many successful repetitions. But the skill is rarely performed under such stationary conditions in a game, so blocked practice does not transfer well to game conditions. The coach should create practice situations with unpredictable events before players encounter the unpredictability of the full game.

How Does This Information Apply to My Coaching Tasks?

Taken together, the preceding information makes a remarkably cohesive body of knowledge. There are five converging lines of evidence, and this convergence makes the recommended applications even more compelling. These concepts apply to three main coaching areas: progressions, drills, and skill testing.

Progressions

At a volleyball clinic I attended, the coach who taught setting recommended a fairly lengthy progression to teach the skill. The progression started with the player kneeling with both hands on the floor in the correct overhead passing position (thumbs 3 centimeters apart and forefingers 8 centimeters apart). Then a ball was placed on the floor, and the player's hands were placed on the ball in the correct overhead passing position. The next position required the player to bend at the waist and bounce the ball repeatedly from the floor to the hands. Other parts of the procedure had partners facing each other while sitting, kneeling, and lying on the floor on their stomachs. It wasn't until progression 15 that the players actually stood facing each other and passed a ball back and forth, and finally on progression 22 three players passed a ball around in a triangle.

Such extensive progressions are an inefficient and ineffective way to teach the motor skills of volleyball. They don't follow the principles of specificity, transfer, and whole practice. Extensive progressions can be used if there is fear or danger, but there isn't much fear or danger associated with setting.

Clearly, progressions must be used to teach motor skills. If I'm teaching my young son how to spike a volleyball, I don't start by having two imposing blockers block every ball he hits, but I don't start with the ball on a spiking tee either. So what rules can be outlined for progressions? There are two:

- Progressions should be limited in number.
- The ones used should be as much like the game of volleyball as possible.

Setting the ball while lying on your stomach does not resemble the game of volleyball. Nixon and Locke (1973) wrote the following about the effectiveness of extensive progressions: "Progression is a near-sacred principle in physical education and is taken most seriously in teacher training. Evidence indicates that the faith . . . may be misplaced. . . . Progressions generally appear not to be significant factors in learning many motor skills" (p. 1217). If you're teaching players to set the ball, the first thing you should have them do is set the ball; if you're teaching them to attack, the first thing you should have them do is attack the ball.

Remember the recommended teaching method? Have them set with emphasis on a key, or have them attack with emphasis on a key, and work through the three or four keys you're using to teach the skill. Don't waste time having them perform activities that do not develop the specific motor programs required for volleyball. There isn't much transfer from lying on the stomach to setting an actual ball. If each day your practices have a greater percentage of transfer to actual game play than those of your opponents, it won't be long until your team is much better than they are.

Drills

Drills, like progressions, must be gamelike. Drills should be designed to develop specific motor programs. Many coaches think that pepper is a great drill to use to teach individual defense. But, in reality, many drills are better than pepper for teaching defense. Marv Dunphy (the 1988 USA Olympic men's team coach) used to say that the best passing drills are pass-set-hit (P-S-H), the best setting drills are P-S-H, the best hitting drills are P-S-H, and the best digging drills are P-S-H and dig. Pepper is not much like volleyball. Marteniuk (1976) says the following about drills:

> Anything less than a game situation, unless very well planned, has the possibility of introducing artificial situations, and complete transfer to the game situation might not occur. When drills are developed, the teacher should carefully consider the way the skills are performed in a game to determine that the drills are as close to the game as possible. (p. 219)

To ensure gamelike drills and increase transfer, coaches should consider these factors when they develop drills:

- The players' positions on the court
- Their movements on the court
- Their orientation to the net
- The sequence of events and the timing of the sequence

- The stimulus to which players react (a coach standing on a table is not the stimulus that a player must react to in a game)
- The natural termination of the ball in play (let most rallies come to a natural termination; don't catch the ball)

Skill Testing

Lawther (1977) wrote, "We have not yet been able to find any means of evaluation of dual or team-sport ability which even approaches the validity of expert judgment" (p. 223). This statement means that we can't really know how well players will play until we put them in a game. For that reason, traditional skills tests should not be the most important element used in team selection. Instead find out who can play the best by watching the players play.

In Super Bowl XXI between the New York Giants and the Denver Broncos, 10 free agents (at that time, all free agents were players who were not considered good enough, coming out of college, to be drafted) started for the Giants (out of 25 starters), and 6 free agents started for the Broncos. Only 6 first-round draft choices started for both teams (out of 50 starters). If the NFL, with all its sophisticated tests and other resources, does no better than this in selecting its players, what can be concluded? The best conclusion is that motor programs are specific and a 40-yard dash test won't tell much about how good a football player is. Neither will a vertical jump test tell much about how good a volleyball player is. You have to use your expertise to subjectively evaluate play.

How Do I Improve My Athletes' Responses?

Coaches should organize practices so that athletes experience many successful responses. (Passing, serving, or spiking a ball are some examples of responses.) Success can be increased by properly scheduling work and rest during practice, not pushing beyond appropriate levels of physical fatigue, and using mental practice.

How Many Minutes Should a Drill Last?

The main question here is, how should work and rest in practice be distributed? If a coach wants to practice serve reception for 30 minutes, how should the time be scheduled? Would it be better to do all 30 minutes at once (massed practice) or to break the time up into smaller blocks, maybe 10 minutes each (distributed practice)? Researchers have studied similar questions for almost 90 years. There have been inconsistencies in the basic findings, but recent evidence suggests that massed practice reduces both the performance and the learning of a motor skill (Lee & Genovese, 1988).

So the best procedure is to provide distributed types of practice. For example, smaller bouts of serve reception would be better than one long 30-minute session. And instead of simply inserting rests between serve reception practices, have the players practice other activities (like serving or spiking). This system realizes the advantages of both distributed practice (no depressed performance or learning) and massed practice (many opportunities to respond).

How Tired Should Players Be?

Many coaches start practice with long warm-ups, ladders or "suicides" (various running patterns), and other physically demanding routines that produce physical fatigue. When I first started coaching, I had my athletes go through a 45-minute circuit-training program before every practice. We were fit, but could we play? (Actually, we were never very good until I stopped the routine.) Research indicates that physical fatigue reduces both performance and learning. Some coaches argue that athletes have to play when they are fatigued, so they need to learn skills when they are fatigued. However, research has found that this procedure is not justified. It appears that practice under ideal conditions is best for learning, regardless of the conditions under which the task is to be performed. So the best place for circuits, ladders, and most fitness activities is near the end of practice, probably just before the cool-down. Of course, practices can still be demanding, but heavy fatigue reduces learning.

Can Players Think About the Game and Get Better?

Research has consistently shown that mental practice can aid in the learning of motor skills, and mental practice is probably best when it is combined with a relaxation program. Sport psychology has made excellent use of routines that combine relaxation and visual imagery. Effective mental practice has these six critical features:

- Mental practice is best when combined with physical practice.
- The performance environment (gym, crowd, etc.) should be visualized when the athlete mentally practices.
- The skill should be performed mentally in its entirety.
- The skill should be rehearsed mentally as being performed successfully.
- The mental practice should be at or near the actual rate of performance.
- Athletes should concentrate on imagining how the action feels.

A coach must realize that the ability to profit from mental practice has to be learned, just like any other skill. As such, it must be practiced; skill development takes time. Because mental practice is difficult to learn, coaches who want to teach it to their teams are advised to read some of the numerous available resources or seek help from someone versed in the procedure. (See chapter 2 for more on mental practice.)

What Information Should Players Receive?

Information obtained after a response, called information feedback, is generally viewed as the most important variable for determining learning, except for practice itself. The following principles will assist coaching.

• The information presented must not overload the information-processing ability of the athletes. Coaches who do not use keys (like the ones discussed on pages 6-7) are more likely to overload players than those who do use them.

• Two types of information can be given: knowledge of results (e.g., That was a straight-down spike) and knowledge of performance (e.g., Your four-step approach was perfect that time). Because knowledge of performance is not easy for the learner to obtain alone, it is especially important for the coach to provide knowledge of performance in the early stages, when the learner has not yet developed an internal standard of correct performance.

• It helps if the coach has playing experience. Hoffman (1983) found that the teacher's analytic proficiency is influenced more by experience with a skill than by the highly organized formal training programs often received in a university education. So it is a good idea for volleyball coaches to learn how to play volleyball.

The primary role of information feedback is to allow the learner to evaluate the response. It provides a framework of reference so that the athlete can detect response errors and attempt to correct them.

Information feedback also performs an important motivational function. Positive information is a great motivator. When players are observed during a break in practice, they are almost always spiking or trying to spike the ball, and they are rarely working on blocking. One reason for this is that positive information is readily available in spiking but very difficult to obtain in blocking. So the information gained from spiking performance is sufficient to maintain practice behaviors (they practice spiking even during breaks) for long periods of time. Players enjoy practices in which they get to spike. Remember how Marv Dunphy recommended the pass-set-hit drills? Coaches should use the players' love of spiking to their advantage when they organize practices.

Players also like practices in which they get lots of positive feedback, because positive feedback is very motivating. So coaches should do everything they can to increase positive feedback in practice. The USA men's team does this in two main ways: setting goals for drills and building in competition.

Goals for Drills

Many coaches like to run very precise practices and schedule exact time periods for each phase of practice. For example, a coach might say something like this: "OK, you know how important serve reception is to our succcess, so I want you to spend the next 15 minutes working on it. Get after it! Work hard!" But players don't work very hard under these conditions, and when they finish they really have no idea how they performed. A much more desirable procedure would be to give the players a goal. For example, say to each player: "I want you to pass 50 balls, and when you finish tell me how many out of the 50 were perfect." Players work harder under these conditions, and when they finish, they know exactly how they have performed. An additional possibility is to say that the team on defense will remain on defense until it beats the offense a certain number of times (or maybe a certain number of times in a row). Now if I defeat you in 2 minutes and it takes you 7 minutes to defeat me, I know that my performance was very good. I know, because I received information feedback.

Competition

Another way to increase information feedback is to make drills competitive. Many observers believe that the USA men's team is the most competitive team in the world, and they are the most competitive team in the world day after day after day. Most other international teams choose the times they will compete, but the USA men are always on. They compete so well because virtually everything they do in practice is competitive, and you can't be competitive without goals for your drills. When players compete in practice, they learn to compete, and they also receive more information. They know whether they have won or lost.

Opportunity to Respond

At the beginning of this section the following statement was made: Information feedback is generally viewed as the most important variable for determining learning, except for practice itself. You need practice trials in order to have information feedback. Several studies have shown that the number of times a player practices a skill (at an appropriate difficulty level) is the best predictor of improvement. So coaches should maximize the number of practice trials, or the number of opportunities to respond. There are four main ways to do this:

- ***Skill warm-up***. Instead of starting each practice with a warm-up that requires the players to jog around in circles, start the warm-up with ball-handling drills. The drills do not have to be intense; they can be at a level that allows gradual warm-up. After this game-specific warm-up, add stretching activities (to guard against injury). The extra 10 minutes spent on ball handling will give you an advantage over teams that warm up by running around in circles.

- ***Tutoring***. In a tutoring session, the coach and one, two, or three players work together to practice a specific skill. Because only a few players are there, each player gets numerous opportunities to respond and receives considerable feedback. Virtually every practice should be preceded by a tutoring session, and it doesn't hurt to end every practice with one.

- ***Small groups***. A certain amount of practice should include six-on-six gamelike drills, but when players play six-on-six, each has fewer chances to play the ball. It makes sense to schedule a number of small-group games, like doubles or triples. If a team of 12 players is divided into three games of doubles, each athlete plays the ball three times as often as when they are playing six-on-six.

- ***Wash games, or in-a-rows***. Bill Neville and Doug Beal devised many practice situations in which their players had to win two—or sometimes three, four, five, or more—rallies in a row. The routine was as follows: Every time a ball was served and the rally terminated, a coach would immediately throw another ball into play. If the objective was to win two in a row, the team that won the first rally would also have to win the second rally. If first one team was successful and then the other, then no points were scored and it was a "wash." The goal can be any number of in-a-rows, so if the goal is to win five in a row, then after the serve, four balls would successively be thrown into play (as long as the same team kept winning the rallies). In this system, the extra balls thrown into play provide many more opportunities for players to respond.

Using all four of these procedures can have a dramatic cumulative effect that gives a team a real advantage over other teams. Try them!

PUTTING MOTOR LEARNING TO WORK FOR YOU

The examples in the ''Motor Learning Concerns in Volleyball'' section showed how a coach can use motor learning concepts to benefit the players. In this section I sketch a model practice (in which the players learn a new skill and practice three old skills) that emphasizes many of these concepts. An outline for the practice is included in Figure 1.2.

Starting Practice

Develop a regular routine for starting practice. Having a formal beginning tells players that practice is serious and important. For example, you might use a whistle to start practice and ask the players to stand on a line in front of the blackboard, where any necessary announcements can be placed and where the daily practice should be outlined.

Players should not stretch their muscles until they are warm, so start practice with easy ball-handling drills. Have the players pick a partner and get a ball for some ball-handling drills (opportunities to respond) that are progressively more difficult and eventually cause a light sweat. Because the first part of practice is devoted to teaching, the warm-up should not be too vigorous. Warm-up should be followed by stretching.

Teaching New Skills

When you teach a new skill, arrange the team so that everyone can see and hear. Take a few minutes to explain and demonstrate the skill. Begin

- 2:00: Lineup, announcements.
- 2:05: Warm-up.
- 2:15: Introduce new skill (blocking).
- 2:45: Serve and serve reception practice (doubles ladder).
- 3:20: Transition hitting (six-on-six, four in a row).
- 4:00: Jump training, warm-down.
- 4:15: Lineup, termination of practice.

Figure 1.2 A model practice outline.

by explaining why the skill is important. In this model practice, the team is going to work on a difficult read-and-react blocking skill, so give the players some reasons why they are going to learn it.

The skill should be demonstrated by someone who can illustrate the important aspects. The first demonstration should be fairly brief and include five or six repetitions of the whole skill. Have the athletes watch from two vantage points. In the case of the read-and-react block, they should view the demonstrator from the front and the side, as these two angles give the clearest picture of what is required in the skill.

Present the keys the players will need to practice this skill. (Normally you should preassess the players' ability to perform the skill before selecting and presenting keys, but for this model practice, the players have no previous experience with this skill.) The first key involves watching the flight of the passed ball and then the setter (ball, setter, ball, hitter). During the first demonstration, have them focus on this aspect.

Have the players practice the skill. As they practice, give feedback (mostly knowledge of performance, e.g., That was perfect, you watched the setter set the ball just the way you should) on only the first key. Try to be positive and compliment effort. You may need to show the key again, and periodically you should ask the athletes to repeat what you've said and done.

When the players have achieved some success at the first key, repeat the process. Demonstrate again, but this time ask the athletes to attend to another aspect of the demonstration. Have the players practice again, and give feedback on the second key. You may need to remind a few athletes of the first key, but emphasize the current objective.

As discussed earlier, you should have your athletes practice on the whole skill, with very few progressions. Because blocking is difficult to learn, it isn't necessary to have the players block live spikes immediately, but the initial drills, like the game of volleyball, should have a ball in play. After three or four keys have been presented (you don't want to overload information-processing ability), and after the whole skill has been practiced with limited gamelike progressions, gamelike drills, and feedback on the keys, terminate this phase of practice. The athletes will need to practice the skill again and again on future days, for performances are still far from perfect. Answer any questions that arise, allow athletes a water break, and move on to the next phase of practice.

Reviewing Skills

Two of the skills that should be practiced every day are serving and serve reception. In this model practice, a round of doubles ladder is used for serve and serve reception practice. The doubles ladder is like a free throw ladder in basketball or a challenge ladder in tennis. The players are listed in order of ability, and players can challenge those above them and take their places on the ladder if they are victorious. Today the team has been divided into three groups of four, and the players will play doubles on three courts (yes, we are lucky enough to have three courts on which to practice). In each group of four, everyone plays doubles with everyone else. Thus, there are three matchups: 1 and 2 versus 3 and 4; then 1 and 3 versus 2 and 4; and finally 1 and 4 versus 2 and 3. Scores for each player are kept for all three matches. After all the matches for the day are over, the top players (based on the points they have accumulated) in Groups 2 and 3 move up a group, and the bottom players in Groups 1 and 2 go down a group.

The doubles ladder provides lots of opportunities to serve and serve receive. The coach can throw an extra ball into the game when a rally has terminated (as in the in-a-row routine) to provide even more repetitions. The doubles ladder is gamelike and competitive, the coach can give feedback as the players play, and the players receive other informational feedback because they know how well they do in the pairings. Games to 15 points (rally scoring) in each of the three matchups take my team about 30 minutes. You will, of course, want to find out how long your team requires.

After the doubles ladder, the team works on transition hitting in a six-on-six format. The drill for this model practice is a simple in-a-row game. The team on offense must win the serve reception and three more rallies in a row. Each rotation is allotted 5 minutes to accomplish the goal, and if the team doesn't finish in the allotted time, the teams rotate and the defense scores a point. If they do finish, the offense scores a point and the teams rotate. The time required to finish is recorded. Now the team that was on defense goes on offense and tries to beat that time.

The drill has many of the same advantages as the doubles ladder. There are lots of opportunities to respond, it is a game, it is competitive, and there is feedback because the players know how well they do in the matchups. An assistant can keep statistics on hitting or other aspects during the drill, and if a certain rotation always fails to finish on time, the coach will have an indication of which rotations are weak and need special attention.

Conditioning

The previous drills will have taken approximately 2 hours. It is time to do jump training, interval running, or other fitness activities. Next will come warm-down and the final lineup before practice ends.

Applying Motor Learning Principles

That's all there is to it! A quote from *In Search of Excellence* by Peters and Waterman (1982) expresses how I feel after presenting these ideas. Peters and Waterman teach classes about successful businesses and the traits these businesses employ. Sometimes they have problems communicating this information to their students. They write:

> The traits are obvious. Presenting the material to students who have no business experience can lead to yawns. "The customer comes first, second, third we say." "Doesn't everyone know that?" is the implied (or actual) response. On the other hand seasoned audiences usually react with enthusiasm. They know that this material is important. . . . They are heartened that the "magic" of a P&G [Procter & Gamble] and IBM is simply getting the basics right, not possessing twenty more IQ points per man or woman. (p. 17)

The few basic motor learning principles that we have outlined are important. Did they lead to yawns or enthusiasm? The magic is in getting them right, in applying them properly. The USA men's team follows these principles and wins gold medals. Try them and see how you do!

KEYS TO SUCCESS

■ **Goal presentation**
- **Athletes have a limited ability to process information, so help them remember information and learn faster by using demonstrations, keys, and feedback about the keys.**
- **Present small amounts of information at a steady rate—not too much and not too fast.**

■ **Motor program development**
- **Make sure that your athletes develop the specific motor programs required for playing volleyball. There isn't much transfer from one motor task to another.**
- **Practice skills as a whole rather than in parts.**
- **Limit the number of progressions and keep them gamelike; make drills competitive and gamelike.**

- **Improving responses**
  - Have players encounter skills under ideal conditions: Schedule practices that have a pleasing distribution of practice time and that do not promote heavy fatigue.
  - Teach players the proper methods of mental practice.

- **Giving information feedback**
  - Make certain that there are numerous opportunities to respond and lots of feedback about those opportunities. Do everything you can to increase practice attempts and meaningful information feedback.

REFERENCES AND RESOURCES

Coaching wisdom from "the Wizard." (1988, May/June). *American Coach*, p. 4.

Engerbretson, D. (1979, late season). Parents, kids and fly rods. *Fly Fisherman*, pp. 22-27.

Gallwey, W. (1974). *The inner game of tennis*. New York: Random House.

Gentile, A. (1972). A working model of skill acquisition with application to teaching. *Quest*, **17**, 3-23.

Henry, F. (1958). Specificity vs. generality in learning motor skills. *College Physical Education Proceedings*, **61**, 126-128.

Hoffman, S. (1983). Clinical diagnosis as a pedagogical skill. In T. Templin & J. Olson (Eds.), *Teaching in physical education* (pp. 35-45). Champaign, IL: Human Kinetics.

Lawther, J. (1977). *The learning of physical skills*. Englewood Cliffs, NJ: Prentice Hall.

Lee, T., & Genovese, E. (1988). Distribution of practice in motor skill acquisition: Learning and performance effects reconsidered. *Research Quarterly for Exercise and Sport*, **59**, 277-287.

Marteniuk, R. (1976). *Information processing in motor skills*. New York: Holt, Rinehart & Winston.

Nixon, J., & Locke, L. (1973). Research on teaching physical education. In R. Travers (Ed.), *Second handbook of research on teaching* (pp. 1210-1242). Chicago: Rand McNally.

Orlick, T., Partington, J., & Salmela, J. (1982). *Mental training for coaches and athletes*. Ottawa, ON: Sport in Perspective and The Coaching Association of Canada.

Peters, T., & Waterman, R. (1982). *In search of excellence: Lessons from America's best-run companies.* New York: Harper & Row.

Salmoni, A., Schmidt, R., & Walter, C. (1984). Knowledge of results and motor learning: A review and critical appraisal. *Psychological Bulletin, 95,* 355-386.

Schmidt, R. (1975). *Motor skills.* New York: Harper & Row.

CHAPTER 2

Sport Psychology: Improving Performance

Martin Gipson
University of the Pacific

Steve Lowe*
University of Wisconsin–Madison

Thom McKenzie
San Diego State University

On October 22, 1988, the University of Wisconsin's women's volleyball team lost 15-4, 15-6, 15-9 to Ohio State University at Ohio State. This match followed a

---

*Steve Lowe was the head coach, women's volleyball, at the University of Wisconsin, Madison. He is now deceased.

loss at Indiana University the previous night, in which Wisconsin also played poorly. At the end of the Ohio State match, the Wisconsin coaches were understandably frustrated with their team's performance, but their words to the players in the locker room did not reflect this. The coaches made no mention of any shortcomings in team or individual play and instead simply said that Ohio State had been "hot" that night. After the team showered, the coaches and players went to dinner. The atmosphere at dinner was light; everyone laughed, joked, and in general enjoyed each other's company.

At practice the following Monday, the Wisconsin coaches analyzed the previous two losses and identified serve reception, blocking, and serving as Wisconsin's primary weaknesses. The next opponent would be the University of Minnesota, a team that used the jump serve and thus was a special threat to Wisconsin's serve reception weakness. Minnesota was an especially intimidating opponent because it was a Top 20 team with a 15-5 record, whereas Wisconsin was 11-11. The coaches concentrated on the three priority weaknesses in practices that week, and on Saturday Wisconsin beat Minnesota at Minnesota by 15-13, 5-15, 9-15, 15-7, and 15-9. Wisconsin players and coaches were overjoyed, and in the locker room after the match the coaches praised the players for their improved execution in the three priority skill areas.

WHY SPORT PSYCHOLOGY IS IMPORTANT

Sport psychology is the science dedicated to understanding (a) the psychological factors that lead to maintaining and improving performance in sport and exercise settings and (b) the psychological effects of participation in sport and exercise. As such, it is a basic aspect of all coaches' effectiveness, whether they have studied psychology or not. Consider the example. What the Wisconsin coach did was apply *formative feedback*; that is, he withheld criticism of his players until a time when they had an opportunity to correct their deficiencies. This procedure, developed by Don Tosti of the Vanguard Consulting Group, is one of many concepts of psychology that volleyball coaches and players can use to improve team performance. Coaches may or may not criticize players after a loss. Either way they are trying to influence players' performance, and either way they have an effect on the players, helpful or harmful. Coaches who know more about psychology will be more effective in achieving the desired changes in player behavior and performance.

Volleyball coaches, like all coaches, are on the firing line—with the players, the players' parents, the athletic directors, and the fans. Coaches are expected to produce results: better volleyball play, better season records, more players who graduate, larger crowds, more fans, and so forth. Their primary means of achieving these goals is through changing their players' behavior and performance. If the players perform well, everyone is happy, and it's easier to win fans and financial support.

Sports participants also have their own goals, such as better skill performance, better self-image, and higher levels of physical conditioning. A coach can better help players achieve personal goals by using sport psychology.

In this chapter we discuss how sport psychology can help the performance of your team, on and off the court. We include many practical suggestions, and we hope you will try at least a few of them. We know volleyball coaches are busy, so we have described techniques that are easy to learn and use.

SPORT PSYCHOLOGY CONCERNS IN VOLLEYBALL

Sport psychology concerns many issues that are relevant to the performance of a volleyball team. This chapter addresses two major concerns of volleyball coaches: helping players achieve consistent quality performances and coaching effectively in practices and matches. Our discussion of achieving consistent quality performances focuses on areas players implement on their own with your guidance, such as appropriate mental preparation, self-teaching and correction, stress reduction, and confidence enhancement, whereas our discussion of effective coaching focuses on daily coaching activities, such as effectively using feedback and praise, communicating instructions, and setting rules and goals.

We present procedures and techniques that apply to problems coaches must deal with daily. Some of the techniques will be familiar to you; others will be new. The procedures and techniques we recommend are not the only ones that could be used effectively, but they are ones that have been shown to be effective in research, and they are practical for use in daily volleyball coaching.

Improving Consistency of Quality Performance

Consistency of quality performance is a fundamental characteristic of an effective player. Some players demonstrate good skills in practice, and some players have an occasional great game, but a coach needs players who play well consistently in matches. A coach can use five avenues to achieve more consistent play: mental preparation, videotape feedback, stress management, increased self-confidence, and improved leadership from players.

Mentally Preparing for Matches

Mental preparation can involve activities like focusing attention on matches, becoming relaxed, using positive self-talk, and visualizing the successful performance of skills. But mental preparation is not a replacement for working on volleyball skills, developing a team's ability to carry out tactics, implementing a conditioning program, or any of the other kinds of hard work involved in developing a successful team. Mental preparation may help a team when it has developed individual and team skills, but most of the assistance the science of sport psychology can offer coaches is in improving the ways in which they work to develop those skills.

The crux of mental preparation has been summarized by Orlick (1986):

In competition the ideal mental state includes being able to:

1. Focus appropriately—attend to what is relevant, the here and now.
2. Deal with distractions—leave your problems outside the gym.
3. Think positively—you must expect good things to happen . . . if good things are ever going to happen. The most important mental state is confidence—belief in yourself, your abilities, and your teammates.
4. Extend your limits—push yourself to the physical limit of your abilities. (p. 16)

The first two elements of this mental state deal with attention and concentration; the second two involve what players expect of themselves. Orlick proposes that consistent play comes from, first, paying attention to action and events pertinent to a match and ignoring what is not relevant and, second, expecting to do very well. The trick, of course, is in achieving these things.

Players can practice four techniques to help achieve a properly prepared mental state:

1. Visually rehearse the performance of skills that must be executed well during a match.
2. Visually and verbally rehearse paying attention to the cues relevant to performing those skills.
3. Say positive things to themselves about the skills they perform in a match.
4. Tell themselves to extend their efforts to the very limits of their skills and abilities.

To develop and maintain a prepared mental state, a player should do some or all of these regularly before a match, during a match, and after a mistake or distraction (Orlick, 1986). Players with consistent ways of preparing for a match generally perform more consistently.

Visual rehearsal involves simply visualizing the correct performance of a volleyball skill. It can be based on how a skill looks from a player's own point of view (internal perspective) or from the point of view of someone watching (external perspective). Players can visualize performances they recall directly or performances they have watched on videotape; in either case it is preferred that they visualize their own good performances, not someone else's.

Players can rehearse paying attention to relevant cues by visualizing the events that precede the performance of a skill. For example, a serve receiver might visualize the flight of the ball from the time a server tosses it to the moment it strikes the passer's arms. Players can learn to attend to cues by calling out relevant events as they occur during practice. Serve receivers could say "ball" when they see the volleyball being served and "pass" as the ball makes contact with their arms (see Ziegler, 1987). After a little practice, players can carry out such sequences silently, but they should still work at paying attention to the right cues.

To improve their ability to say positive things about their play and to push themselves to their limits, ask players to propose several *positive* statements about how they are going to play, concentrate, give 100 percent, push themselves, and so forth. Then have them begin using these statements; this will allow players to direct themselves to better play, and it will also reduce the time they spend talking negatively to themselves, worrying, and thinking self-defeating thoughts.

Work with your players individually and as a team to get them to implement these steps. Go over what players plan to visually rehearse and say to themselves. Doing so ensures that the players are mentally preparing in a way that benefits the team's performance, and it lets them know that these procedures are part of your immediate priorities. After players begin to use mental preparation techniques, you will need to regularly prompt their use before and during matches; otherwise players will gradually conclude that mental preparation is no longer important to you.

In summary, one key to your team's consistent performance is for each player to have a consistent way to prepare for matches and to deal with distractions and poor performances during matches. For more information on implementing a mental preparation program, see the book *Psyching for Sport* (Orlick, 1986). We strongly suggest that you obtain copies for your players and *Coaches Training Manual to Psyching for Sport* for yourself.

Self-Teaching and Self-Correcting With Videotape

Video feedback can be used to develop consistent player performance. There are three types of video feedback: corrective video, for identifying and eliminating performance deficits; positive video, for providing players with models of correct performance for visualization and for motivation; and motivational video, for motivating players.

Corrective video	$\longrightarrow$	Identify and eliminate performance errors
Positive video	$\longrightarrow$	Identify and prompt correct performance and motivate players
Motivational video	$\longrightarrow$	Motivate players

Corrective feedback involves players' reviewing their performances on videotape to identify shortcomings. If you already use video feedback, this is most likely how you use it. It is most effective when a player already performs most elements of a skill correctly. Make sure that you or an assistant is present to cue the player on what to look for. Few people enjoy watching themselves make mistakes, so players may not gain as much as you would hope from this approach.

Positive videotape feedback (Dowrick, 1983) (also termed video feedforward) uses edited tapes from practices and matches that show individual players shots of themselves performing targeted skills properly—no mistakes are shown. These tapes can help players see more clearly the proper way to perform a skill; these tapes can also lead to improved performances by providing players with a convincing model of themselves performing well. Positive video is used with players who perform most elements of a skill incorrectly to show them clearly what to do and to provide a model for their visualizations of correct performances. It is used with skilled players to increase their confidence by showing them that they indeed can perform a skill well. It is best for players to study positive video on their own; you have already decided that what is on the tape represents a good performance.

Positive tapes are made individually for each player. The coach selects a priority skill for the player to work on and sits down with a person familiar with videotape editing to watch videotapes from that player's matches and practices. The coach points out several skill performances that are appropriately performed, and the editor copies them onto a short tape. To make proper form easier for players to see, you can have every third skill performance copied in slow motion. The tapes, usually 5 minutes in length, should show only appropriate skill performances.

When watching these tapes, players should try to describe the elements of the skill that they believe are important to watch; if you are present, you should reinforce and elaborate on what players say. You should also prompt players—both during viewings and at practices and matches—to actually use targeted skills as shown on these tapes.

Motivational videotapes help players psych up for matches and help prompt correct skill performances. They should be edited individually for each player and should include 1 or 2 minutes from positive videotapes produced for the player and 1 or 2 minutes of team footage from matches the team has won. Dubbing the tape with music selected by the player can increase the tape's motivational effectiveness. A tape can then be given to each player, who can decide whether to watch the tape before matches.

Controlling Stress

Stress contributes significantly to inconsistency in players' performance on the court. Stress can also increase the chances of injury for some players. So coaches need to recognize stress-producing circumstances and help players reduce stress.

Volleyball players are exposed to all of the stresses of ordinary life—the loss of friends, the ending of romantic relationships, and the loss of jobs or other sources of financial support. These can be very important negative influences on a player's performance. Other sources of player stress are specific to sports and to volleyball in particular. Table 2.1 lists sources of stress specific to volleyball. Use this list to anticipate the stress level of your players in a match or tournament. As a coach, you can control

Table 2.1

Sources of Stress for Volleyball Players

Matches

Intense, high-level competition

Large, noisy crowds

Extremes of heat, cold, and humidity on the court

Falling behind in a game or match

A close score

Officials' calls against the team

Being constantly yelled at by opponent players or fans

Being constantly yelled at by own coach or teammates

Making a series of playing errors

Expecting to be substituted for at the first error

The injury of a key player

Being asked to start unexpectedly

Being asked to make game point or to serve at game point

Practices

Long, repetitive practices

Practices that occur over long periods of days without a break

Heat, cold, and humidity

Constant criticism from coaches and other players

Drills that players cannot succeed at

Very early or very late practice times

Travel

Very early and very late departure and arrival times

Long stopovers or many stops during a trip

Missed flights, late buses

Crowding and noise on buses and airplanes

Loss of sleep

Poor food

Being away from home

Separation from family and friends

Uncomfortable rooms

Dirty clothes

Lack of things to do or a lack of choice of things to do with free time

Lack of free time

Incompatible roommates

Additional Sources of Player Stress

Coaches who are not clear about whom they consider to be the better and weaker players on a team

Coaches who are not clear about how they evaluate players, decide who starts, and so forth

Coaches who are not objective in evaluating players, deciding who starts, and so forth

Not knowing who opponents are going to be or where or when competitions will be played or minimize some sources of stress; for example, you can refrain from constantly criticizing players and their performances. Other sources of stress are not under your control, but you can help players handle the stress.

Coaches and sport psychologists alike have long been taught that some stress and anxiety can help performance but that too much stress can hurt it. This has made it difficult to decide just when and if stress is too high and when to do something about it. But recent evaluations of the effects of stress in sports have shown that stress from fear, apprehension, and other negative feelings never helps performance (Neiss, 1988). Any players who are under stress or are afraid—afraid of losing, of getting injured, of large crowds, and so forth—can benefit from relaxation.

We suggest using either of two types of relaxation techniques: (a) muscle relaxation such as through stretching and progressive muscle relaxation and (b) breathing relaxation such as through diaphragmatic breathing. Progressive muscle relaxation is an active method by which a player can learn to regulate stress. The player sits or lies in a quiet area and sequentially tightens and relaxes a number of muscle groups; the player learns to recognize and reduce muscle tension that is associated with stress. Step-by-step instructions can be found in introductory sports medicine texts such as *Modern Principles of Athletic Training* (Arnheim, 1985).

A new, simple breathing relaxation technique called *respiratory manipulation training* can also help players relax. It's easy to learn and takes only a minute to implement. Using it, a coach or player can prompt relaxation during a time-out or even during play by saying "relax" (see Longo & vom Saal, 1984, and Longo, Clum, & Yaeger, 1988).

**What to Say When Introducing
Respiratory Manipulation Training to Players***

[NOTE: Words in brackets are slightly adapted versions of instructions to the group leader.]

Now we are going to learn a relaxation technique called respiratory manipulation training. This technique is a very effective yet simple relaxation technique to learn and use. Its effectiveness comes from two sources. First, you will be exercising your diaphragm. This muscle will use up a lot of energy. By using up the energy, you will feel relaxed, sort of like after you have exercised a great deal and feel the "let-down," at-peace-with-the-world feeling. Second,

---

(continued)

Respiratory Manipulation *(continued)*

---

while you practice respiratory manipulation training, you will be building up the carbon dioxide concentrations in your blood (again, like when you exercise a lot). This build-up of carbon dioxide has a tranquilizing effect on your nervous system and thus reduces your arousal level.

Respiratory manipulation training is a breathing technique. First, you must learn how to breathe. Many people do not breathe properly. Let's all breathe deeply and slowly. Put your hands on your sides and breathe from the diaphragm. If you are breathing properly, your hands should be moving out with each inhalation and in during the exhalation. [Now the leader demonstrates breathing properly and makes sure all group members are breathing correctly.]

The second part of the respiratory manipulation training involves expelling all the air from your lungs. Refrain from breathing at this point, for as long as you can. When you can no longer refrain from breathing, inhale and experience respiratory relief. (*NOTE*: Some individuals must take a short, quick breath, followed by a deep breath, to experience the relief.) [The leader demonstrates and the group practices until all members are skilled. Next the leader demonstrates the combined procedure of two deep breathing cycles, a full exhalation, maximum voluntary respiratory arrest, and then inhalation and respiratory relief. The leader repeats the procedure.]

[After the group has practiced the sequence continuously for 20 minutes, ask each member to say the word "RELAX" or "CALM" with each exhalation for an additional 5 minutes. Ask the players to practice for 15 minutes each day, and encourage them to use the technique whenever they feel stressed, reminding them to use the cue word "RELAX" or "CALM" with each exhalation.]

From A Psychosocial Treatment Intervention for Recurrent Genital Herpes: An Investigation of Psychoneuroimmunology (pp. 179-181) by D.J. Longo, 1986, unpublished doctoral dissertation, Virginia Polytechnic Institute and State University, Blacksburg, VA. (University Microfilms No. 86-25803). Copyright 1987 by David Joseph Longo. Adapted by permission.

Building Self-Confidence

Confidence is built through success in practices and competition and recognition for those successes. The importance of establishing a positive learning environment, as described later in this chapter, cannot be stressed enough. Players' confidence is enhanced when they know they are performing well, and this depends in large part on coaches' and assistants' paying attention to and appreciating players' efforts and accomplishments. Assistant coaches or other support staff can also help by passing on positive comments they have heard the head coach say about players.

Coaches can help players who are low in self-confidence establish what their strengths and contributions to the team are by recording those assets. Begin by asking players to talk or write about their strengths, not only on the court, but off it as well. Also, have them talk or write about the good things that have happened to them and the positives they have in their lives. Once they overcome inhibitions about seeming egotistical, players enjoy this process. Keep a permanent record in your coaching notebook of what the players cite as their strengths so that you can remind yourself and them of these strengths when they are depressed or low in self-confidence.

Positive Visualization.   Tell players to become relaxed through one of the relaxation methods described earlier and then to recall a match where they played exceptionally well. Tell them to describe the key feelings and plays that occurred in this match and to have someone record those descriptions so they'll have a record of the performance to refer to. You also may have players watch one or more positive videotapes of themselves. Players can then visualize these performances on their own before going into a match. This helps their confidence by reminding them that they can indeed play well.

Positive Self-Talk and Coping With Performance Errors.   Coaches will hear players say degrading things to themselves. By saying those things, players diminish their self-confidence and prompt themselves to perform poorly. But players can learn to monitor their self-talk to reduce the negative self-talk and increase the positive statements. To do this, players should practice positive statements that they can repeat comfortably (e.g., "I'm quick," "I'm strong," "I'm confident"). Players who constantly practice positive self-talk are prompting themselves to play well, have less time for negative self-talk, and are more self-confident.

Players can also learn to talk rationally to themselves. For example, players may decide early in a match that they don't feel well and then think, "This isn't my day." This is another self-prompt for a poor performance. Players can learn to change such self-talk, for example, thinking, "I feel sluggish, but it is good that I recognize this now so that I can change it. I'm going to move quicker and get myself going." Such self-talk prompts the desired performance and makes it more likely to occur.

Some players say negative things to themselves when they make an error; others blame teammates, the opponent players, the coach—anyone but themselves. Still other players obsess about the error long after it has occurred. None of these responses is helpful, and all place players in danger of committing still more errors. Instead of criticizing themselves or others after making an error, players should use errors to prompt themselves on what to do on the next play—just as you would instruct them. For example, after missing a pass the player can say, "On the next serve reception I'm going to be in the correct position" instead of "You dummy, you've done it again!"

Risk Taking.   Players must be willing to attempt a tough serve or to call for a set at match point, both of which are signs of a confident player. But for players to do this, they must be rewarded for taking risks, even when the outcome is not positive. For example, if a player attempts to serve tough, to go for an ace, and nets instead, that player should be rewarded for taking the risk, not yelled at for missing the serve. Obviously, players should not risk moves that they cannot make, such as trying to smash a hit through two perfectly positioned blockers. But within this guideline, players should be praised for taking risks even when they don't achieve the desired outcome.

Coaches who punish based on the outcome limit player risk taking, because players, like anyone else, avoid doing what they have been punished for doing. When players learn that they will be yelled at if they make a mistake, they also learn to play it safe and just take the sure hit or serve.

Team Leadership and Player-to-Player Communication

Leadership from players is critical to a team's ability to turn around a game or match. Players need to be able to direct their own and their teammates' play effectively when they are not playing well. Such leadership is a skill, and it can be taught. Your example as a leader is your team's first and most important source of information on how to lead. Players and team captains will take their cues from how you behave.

Work with your players as a group to increase the support and direction they give each other on-court. Start by asking each player what he or she would like to hear on-court. Then give examples of how to make a request and give direction on-court (state specifically the behaviors desired from a teammate, such as "Block line when #7 is set" instead of "You missed your blocking assignment") and how to agree and disagree on-court (always acknowledge a request and then concretely state a response without exclaiming, "I'll do it" or "That won't work, she almost never hit line last game''). Your goal is for players to be able to give and receive support and direction without feeling that they are being blamed for problems on the court.

To train captains, use a five-step model of leadership training: Captains can learn to (a) describe what team members should do; (b) model the desired behaviors; (c) determine when players have done what was asked of them; (d) pay attention to and praise the occurrence of the desired behaviors; and (e) determine when playing conditions require a change in individual and team performance (Scott & Podsakoff, 1982). Teach these skills by your example and through individual meetings with the captain. Be sure to prompt the captain to use these skills as they are learned and give feedback when they are used.

Coaching Effectively in Practices and Matches

Imagine having just found out that your team's practice periods have been reduced from last season; you now must decide how to best use the short time available. You know you have a formidable task ahead if your players are to learn the skills you want them to have and do well in competition. You must ensure that your players know what to do, engage them in appropriate skill practice, provide feedback on how they are doing, and if needed, motivate them to try hard and to persist at their task. If you had all the time in the world and three assistants to help, you could get all these things done. Information from the science of psychology suggests the following as the best uses for your limited time and resources.

Creating a Positive and Effective Learning Environment

Plan your practices far in advance as a rule. Write down some long-term goals and refer to them from time to time. Then establish daily practice goals that will achieve your long-term goals, making sure that each practice has a particular focus. Let the players know each day's focus. Make sure your goals for the team, players, and coaches are all realistic ones. Nothing is more aversive than to strive for unattainable goals.

Work hard at giving clear instructions to players. The only effective instruction is the one that gets players to do what you ask of them. When players misunderstand it is easy to become frustrated and blame them, but to be effective you must find other ways to describe what you want. Otherwise players learn that they will be punished if they ask questions, and they won't let you know when your instructions are unclear. Being able to rephrase instructions without becoming angry is a major step toward becoming an effective coach.

This

Coach: Run the play set the way we've practiced it!

Setter: I don't understand! What do you mean by 'the way we practiced it?'

Coach: Set the first hitter on every third set.

Not this

Coach: Run the play set the way we've practiced it!

Setter: I don't understand! What do you mean by 'the way we practiced it?'

Coach: How many times do I have to explain it!

Learn to interact positively with all players. Make sure you pay attention to each player sometime during each practice; it is easy sometimes to forget third-string players. Occasionally use a chart to track players, the quality of your interactions (positive or negative), and the focus of your interactions (e.g., skill success, skill error, lateness, effort) to help make sure you address everyone appropriately. In Table 2.2, for example, we can see that the coach is paying little attention to Harrel and making only negative comments to Odum. After reviewing her chart, this coach may decide to try to give a little more attention to Harrel and to make a positive comment or two to Odum.

Creating a positive learning environment—an environment in which most feedback is positive—promotes players' self-esteem and feelings of well-being. Practices then are not looked at as something to be avoided because of impending punishment but rather as something to look forward to because of the positive reinforcement that will be received. Obviously, coaches must tell players what they do incorrectly. But in an environment that is primarily positive, players are more receptive to criticism because they have learned that this is not the only type of feedback they receive. A good ratio to strive for is four praise statements for every criticism (Daniels & Rosen, 1986).

Providing Effective Feedback to Players in Practices and Matches

We introduced this chapter with a discussion of formative feedback, feedback that is given at a time when players can act on it to improve their performance. For example, if players are criticized immediately after

	White	Harrel	Odum	Carter	Regis	Allen
Table 2.2						
Coach's Chart of Interactions With Players						
Negative (−) or positive (+) comment	−		−	−	−	+
Focus of comment	Arm swing		Ball toss for serve	Approach to net	Back set	Timing on block
Negative (−) or positive (+) comment	−		−	+	+	−
Focus of comment	Arm swing		Ball toss for serve	Arm swing on quick set	Positioning of hands on ball	Arm position on block
Negative (−) or positive (+) comment		−	−	+		+
Focus of comment		Poor effort	Ball toss for serve	Approach to net		Timing on block

a match, there is nothing they can do at that time to change what has happened or to improve for the future. They can only feel guilty or angry at the coach for blaming them. As a result, players may not work as hard as they can in future practices and games, and if they are addressed frequently in this way, they may avoid the coach to escape additional criticism, making the coach's job even more difficult.

On the other hand, players who hear criticism of their performances when they can try to change, such as at the beginning of a practice or during a match, can immediately try to correct the problem. Under these conditions players can see that a coach is trying to improve their performances instead of blaming them for a loss or a shortcoming, and they will pay more attention to what the coach says and even seek out criticism and feedback instead of avoiding it.

The rules of formative feedback are difficult for most coaches to stick to, because making negative comments after a game reduces their own frustration. However, formative feedback is well worth putting into use even beyond its immediate impact in improving player performance. It allows coaches the time to review team performance away from the heat of a match before giving players feedback and criticism, thus assuring more accurate analysis. And it eliminates one major opportunity for negative coaching behaviors, automatically making any coach more positive in dealing with players.

As long as your players have the chance to act on it, they should receive formative feedback as quickly as possible after they attempt a skill or, if possible, concurrent with the attempt. It should be as specific as possible and targeted to the right player. Use short, precise phrases rather than long, complicated descriptions. Players will rarely remember more than three elements given simultaneously in an instruction.

Because so much feedback occurs naturally from skill attempts, it would be counterproductive to stop all your players from practicing just to give formative feedback to one or two. During the course of a practice or game is one opportunity to use motivational feedback (e.g., "Good job!"), feedback that conveys little information but lets players know you approve of their performance. Such feedback can motivate athletes and let them know you care for them.

Formative feedback guides performance

Performance $\longrightarrow$ Feedback $\longrightarrow$ Performance

Motivational feedback praises performance

Performance $\longrightarrow$ Feedback

A large proportion of formative feedback should be positive, indicating that a player is doing a skill or parts of a skill correctly. This lets players know which elements of the skill to repeat when they perform the skill again. Positive feedback is also important because it creates a pleasant environment and engenders good feelings toward the provider. But formative feedback need not always be positive. If it isn't positive, it should be directly related to the skill attempt and should be given matter-of-factly. In the long run it does little good to belittle a player for making repeated errors or for appearing to give mediocre effort. Remember, one long-term goal is for players to become more involved in volleyball. If your environment is too aversive, it could turn them off to both the sport and school.

As a coach you are only one source of formative feedback. Other players and your assistants can give valuable feedback as well. To give useful feedback, one needs to know the critical elements of the skill or strategy to be performed and to know how to present feedback appropriately. You may have to teach other players and assistant coaches to analyze skills or plays and how to give feedback. You may even have to give them feedback on how they provide feedback!

Communicating Effectively During Prematch Meetings, at Time-Outs, and Between Games

Before each meeting have a particular focus. Write it down so you can refer to it later. Before beginning a meeting or time-out, eliminate as many distractions as possible. Don't try to say too many things between games or during time-outs. Players cannot focus on a lot of information during a match, particularly if the information is new and they are under stress. Establish routines for getting water and wiping dry so players can focus on what you tell them.

If the game is close and players are stressed, instruct them to try well-rehearsed and less complex plays. Never expect players to perform skills or plays in a match that they can't do in practice. Have players indicate (e.g., by nodding) that they know what you are asking them to do. Prompt them to focus on the very next skill to be performed when the game begins again. During the match make sure your body language models the behavior you want from the players. Don't expect them to be relaxed and ready to receive the ball if you are grimacing and red-faced on the sideline.

Communicating Effectively During Postgame Meetings and Helping Players Handle Outcomes

Helping players handle outcomes begins with being willing to explain why some players start and why you used the approaches you did for playing opponents. Remember, you set the example. How you handle practices and pre- and postgame meetings teaches players much about how they should cope with wins and losses. Players are much more likely to do as you do than to do as you say.

At postgame meetings avoid blaming players for losses and shortcomings in play. Instead make team and staff members feel that they all are important to the team's success. When the team wins, all members should feel they contributed. The starters will know they contributed because of the time they played and their successes on the court. However, the nonstarters will have made less obvious contributions: They provided the starters with competition in practices, support from the bench, and an occasional opportunity to rest during a match. Both starters and coaches should recognize the contributions of nonstarters when they talk about a team's successes to others, to themselves, and to the nonstarters.

After a loss, the situation is reversed, and the starters might be held solely to blame. You must now communicate to the team that the team lost as a whole and that everyone, including the coaches, holds some responsibility. Let players know there are things to be learned by everyone after losses and wins and that this can't happen if blame is placed on someone in particular.

Whether you win or lose, summarize briefly how the match went in relation to your game plan. Be sure to point out a few specific instances where things went well—even if you have to make them up. Summarize weaknesses in a general manner only. Tell how the next practices will be organized to overcome any apparent weaknesses. End by restating what went well. In all cases, be brief. Most of what you say will be long forgotten by the next practice.

Establishing and Using Team Rules

Your school, conference, and other sport-governing bodies already have rules all athletes must follow. Establish a limited number of additional rules of your own, making sure each one relates to your goals for the team. You may want to involve your players in developing these rules by organizing a discussion about rules around the primary team goal for the season. This will make the purpose of any rule clear and will improve compliance with all rules. In any case, keep your rules realistic. State rules positively so that players know what to do, not just what not to do.

In order for rules to be effective, players must know what the rules are and what the consequences are for both following and breaking them. Make your rules public so that friends and family members also know what is expected of players. Provide prompts for the rules (particularly when a violation is imminent, such as a curfew rule on an important party night that is followed by a district championship), and reinforce your players for following them. Decide in advance what the likely consequences are for rule violations. That way, you can deal with problems without too much anger. Deliver negative consequences quickly and without much display of emotion. Specify the rule that was broken, the penalty, and what the player must do to regain his or her status on the team.

Facilitating Improvement in Players Through Goal Setting

As a coach you are in a powerful position to help your players grow, not only in developing volleyball skills, but also in growing academically, socially, and emotionally. One of the most effective ways you can do this is to teach them the goal-setting process. This process consists of setting goals, making plans to reach these goals, and keeping track of progress made toward reaching the goals. Research provides strong evidence that goal setting is effective in improving athletes' performance (Locke & Latham, 1985), and children as young as 8 years old have been able to use it in schools and sports settings.

Setting goals gives players direction for their actions and standards to measure their progress. You play an important role in helping players set goals. Make sure all goals are realistic. Players should never set goals that they cannot reasonably be expected to achieve; failure to reach goals reduces the chances that players will work hard to achieve new goals in the future. But goals also must not be too easy to achieve, or the players will make little progress. Because you know what is appropriate and possible for a player and a team to attempt, your help with players' goal setting is crucial.

The most difficult part of goal setting is getting started. Set aside part of at least two team meetings for this purpose. At the first meeting, state that you are going to start each individual player on a goal-setting program and explain that goal setting will help them improve as individual players and as a team. Give them an example of how the program will work by providing some team goals. These goals should illustrate the qualities of effective goals: (a) They are specific, having observable and measurable outcomes (e.g., We will have a team hitting percentage of 40 percent in our next match); (b) they are challenging but attainable (Our team hitting percentage for the year will be 40 percent—not 60 percent); and (c) some are long-term (e.g., We will have a win-loss record of 20-10 for this season), and some are short-term (e.g., We will pass at 2.0 in our next match).

At the second meeting explain how each player should go about writing goals. Give players overall team goals with which their goals should mesh. Ask for two goals to begin with, one long-term and one short-term, each related to their performance as players. Long-term goals generally refer to an outcome desired over a season or longer, whereas short-term goals are achievable within a segment of a season, such as during the next match, week, or month. A well-written goal is brief, contains at least one action word (verb), states a specific standard to achieve, and sets a time limit. For example, the long-term goal "In 6 weeks I will pass at 2.0" is much preferable to "I will continue to get better," because the first goal lets players know what they have to do and by when. Without those pieces of information, players have nothing concrete to strive for.

The following statement would be a relevant short-term goal: ''I will practice passing an extra half hour each day for 1 month.'' Make sure all goals are written in a journal so that you can review them.

Arrange to meet with players individually to review and improve their initial goal statements, and then schedule brief monthly individual meetings between you or an assistant and each player to keep the process on track. At these meetings praise progress made toward achieving goals, give advice on how to work toward achieving unmet goals, and help write new goals.

PERSONAL AND SOCIAL DEVELOPMENT OF YOUNG VOLLEYBALL PLAYERS

As a coach working with young volleyball players, you should be concerned with three issues beyond the specifics of coaching. First, recognize that in working with young players you are influencing their development just as parents do. As a coach you serve as a role model for players, especially for the youngest players. A coach who yells at players produces players who yell at each other. A team of players who yell at each other inevitably causes young new players to behave in the same way. In contrast, a coach who is supportive and problem solving–oriented leads players to use these same skills. Coaches should also reinforce desirable behaviors. When coaches see young players behaving in desired, effective ways, they should let the players know that these are the kinds of behaviors they want to see.

Second, because volleyball players in high school and college are maturing from childhood to adulthood, remember that young players' behavior will change as time passes. Effective coaches expect these changes and encourage growth in desirable directions by their instruction, by their example, and by recognizing and praising player maturation. Gradually give players more freedom and responsibility. You are planting the seeds for success; while you are working with young players, you are instilling values and behaviors that will ultimately blossom to benefit both the player and the team.

Third, young players who have primarily negative sports experiences may drop out from volleyball and from other sports as well. It is easy to expect too much from young players, thus insuring that they will constantly fall short and receive much criticism and little praise. Players who are constantly criticized and stressed by their coaches gain little from continuing to participate in volleyball, and they may develop a negative attitude toward sports.

PUTTING SPORT PSYCHOLOGY TO WORK FOR YOU

As in any attempt to try something new in coaching, start gradually in implementing sport psychology techniques. Start with one area where your team has real potential to improve, such as individual skill performance. Then try one technique, such as goal setting, that makes sense to you and that fits easily into the way you work with your team. Start small, perhaps with skill performance goals for just one player, before moving on to the whole team. Then give yourself time to try the goal-setting process with that player and to work systematically and comfortably with the process. Be systematic, and don't expect instant results. It takes time to effectively use a technique you haven't used before. If you're getting results with goal setting and want to try something else new, such as using formative feedback, proceed only when you feel the goal-setting process allows you time to work on your feedback style.

Never try something that doesn't seem easy for you to implement. You'll quickly find that you don't take the time needed to do it properly, and you'll soon drop it altogether. And don't announce to your players that you are starting a sport psychology program. The term *psychology* has negative meanings for many people, and the players may think you are going to psychoanalyze them, or try to read their minds, or otherwise intrude into their personal lives. Remember, you are using principals of sport psychology to be more effective in what you are already doing, that is, helping your team and players perform at a high level and receive the benefits the players desire from participation in volleyball.

The Program of the USA Volleyball Women's National Team

We work as a performance enhancement team for the USA volleyball women's national team. In our work we implement many of the programs we have described in this chapter.

We provide extensive feedback to coaches on (a) their interactions with players during practices and (b) player and team skill performances, based on data collected by observers we trained. We provide consultation on effective strategies for organizing and implementing

---

(continued)

The Program *(continued)*

practices and other team and individual coach interactions with players. We also provide consultation on long-range planning for team activities over an Olympic quadrennium and on a wide range of problems of organization and implementation of team procedures.

We implement an extensive video feedback program for player skill development. We provide players with regular goal-setting sessions; training in leadership skills, the use of mental preparation and self-management strategies; consultation and activities designed to improve self-confidence; help in defining career goals and activities; and preparation for foreign travel, both in terms of such performance variables as jet lag and in terms of culture and language.

KEYS TO SUCCESS

■ To improve quality playing consistency
- Introduce your players to mental preparation through Terry Orlick's book, *Psyching for Sport.*
- Begin implementing one or more of the three forms of videotape feedback.
- Introduce your team to one of the two ways of reducing stress.
- Begin improving your players' self-confidence.
- Develop specific leadership skills in your players.

■ To improve your coaching
- Review and improve your use of goal setting, instructions, and feedback with your team.
- Concentrate on paying attention to your players' successes; you will automatically notice their shortcomings.
- Always remember that you are a model for the behavior of your players.

REFERENCES AND RESOURCES

Arnheim, D. (1985). *Modern principles of athletic training.* St. Louis: Times-Mirror/Mosby.

Daniels, A.C., & Rosen, T.A. (1986). *Performance management*. Tucker, GA: Performance Management.

Dowrick, P.W. (1983). Self-modeling. In P.W. Dowrick & S.J. Biggs (Eds.), *Using video* (pp. 105-124). New York: Wiley.

Locke, E.A., & Latham, G.P. (1985). The application of goal setting to sports. *Journal of Sport Psychology, 7*, 205-222.

Longo, D., Clum, G., & Yaeger, N. (1988). Psychosocial treatment for recurrent herpes. *Journal of Consulting and Clinical Psychology, 56*, 61-66.

Longo, D., & vom Saal, W. (1984). Respiratory relief therapy. *Behavior Modification, 8*, 361-378.

Matheson, D.W. (1978). *Relaxation for the elimination of stress* [Audiotape]. Stockton, CA: University of the Pacific Bookstore.

Neiss, R. (1988). Reconceptualizing relaxation treatment: Psychobiological states in sports. *Clinical Psychology Review, 8*, 139-159.

Orlick, T. (1986). *Psyching for sport*. Champaign, IL: Leisure Press.

Scott, W.E., & Podsakoff, P.M. (1982). Leadership, supervision, and behavior control: Perspectives from an experimental analysis. In Lee Frederiksen (Ed.), *Handbook of organizational behavior management* (pp. 39-69). New York: Wiley.

Seligman, M.E. (1991). *Learned optimism*. New York: Knopf.

Williams, J. (Ed.) (1986). *Applied sport psychology*. Mountain View, CA: Mayfield.

Ziegler, G. (1987). Effects of stimulus cueing on the acquisition of groundstrokes by beginning tennis players. *Journal of Applied Behavior Analysis, 20*, 405-411.

ACKNOWLEDGMENT

The authors acknowledge the assistance of Monica Foster, a PhD candidate in clinical psychology at the University of Mississippi, in the preparation of the manuscript.

CHAPTER 3

Biomechanics: Analyzing Skills and Performance

Jim Coleman
USA National Volleyball Teams Training Center

Kim ColemaNesset
University of California, Davis

Al was 6'6", strong, and very quick. He was a fine quick hitter but had some problems at critical times as a middle blocker. To help him improve, I analyzed his blocking moves by watching videotapes of three hard-fought matches.

He blocked adequately against the middle attack, blocked well against any high set, and blocked fairly well when he had to move to his right on a fast set. However, he blocked poorly when he had to move quickly to his left.

Others made comments about his blocking such as "He seems to be out of control" or "When he gets into trouble, he is off balance," but these observations did not pinpoint his problem. Careful biomechanical analysis identified that Al had a common movement error: He was one-footed. No matter which direction he needed to move along the net, he moved his right foot first.

Thus, he did well when time was not a factor, and he did well when he moved to the right, but quick movements to the left were a disaster. He always made a short step to the right, then attempted to go to the left. Sometimes he crossed over and other times he shuffled. Because he was late and confused, he would end up off balance and out of control.

Movement training, in which he learned to make appropriate initial steps in either direction, corrected many of Al's problems.

WHY BIOMECHANICS IS IMPORTANT

The scenario just described is repeated many times on teams everywhere. Athletes unknowingly violate the principles of efficient movement, and coaches search for solutions.

Biomechanical problems may be solved many ways, but the following three steps should be included: Recognize that there is a problem, identify the biomechanical flaw, and train the athlete to perform the proper biomechanical technique.

BIOMECHANICAL CONCERNS IN VOLLEYBALL

Biomechanics is the study of the physics of movement. Sound biomechanical principles will promote, but not guarantee, outstanding performance of volleyball skills. Generally, athletes following sound biomechanical principles not only perform at a high level but also sustain a minimum number of injuries.

The study of biomechanics is complex. Often scientific biomechanical findings are difficult for the practitioner to understand, to evaluate, and to use. This presentation focuses on basic principles that coaches can easily observe in the gymnasium. These principles involve static or near-static positions rather than complex interactions between linear and angular movements. This discussion is an introduction to, not a comprehensive analysis of, the biomechanics of volleyball.

You need to understand three biomechanical terms: *center of gravity*, *velocity*, and *momentum*. The center of gravity is that point within or near a body about which the weight of the body is evenly distributed or balanced and around which it may be assumed to act. The center of gravity of a human standing erect is near the navel and within the body. The position of the center of gravity changes as the limbs move and as the body bends. For instance, when the human bends forward, the center of gravity moves outside the body to a position approximately in front of the navel.

Velocity is the speed of an object in a specific direction. Momentum is the product of the mass of a body times its velocity. Mass is proportional to weight. When two or more bodies collide, the total momentum of the system must be conserved; no momentum can be lost. For example, when a volleyball is spiked, the velocity of the spiked ball is a complex function that is determined in part by the weight of the spiker, the velocity of the spiker, the velocity of the arm swing, and the point of contact of the spiker's hand on the ball.

This chapter addresses the laws of biomechanics as they relate to volleyball skills. For each skill, a few simple rules are given to illustrate these laws.

Movement From a Static Position

In a number of situations, a volleyball player must react to the stimulus of an oncoming ball. The player's performance depends on a number of factors, including the player's

- position on the court,
- initial body position,
- motivation and anticipation,
- specific reaction time, and
- mechanics of movement.

We will discuss effective court position, initial body position, and mechanics of movement. Anticipation, motivation, and reaction times are topics for other fields of study.

Preparation for Moving Efficiently

The human body is not suited to move equally well in all directions. The body can be positioned to move well in a single direction, such as in a sprinting start. It also can be positioned to move fairly well in two opposing directions, such as when a baseball player leading off a base has equal possibilities of racing to the next base or escaping back to the original base.

However, it is extremely difficult to place a human in position to move efficiently in three directions, such as right, left, or forward. Another three-directional dilemma is that of moving to the right or the left or jumping up. It is nearly impossible to position a human to move adeptly in four or five directions. Decide which directions are important for the primary movements of your players, and then position the players so they can best move quickly in those directions. Do this by following three rules.

Rule One: Limit the number of moves expected from a player.

Place the player on the court in a position that limits the common movements to two or three, at most. For example, place a defensive player at the rear of an area of responsibility rather than in the center of it. In the center (Figure 3.1a) the player may be expected to move four ways, but from the rear, the player is expected to move in only two or three directions (Figure 3.1b).

Positioning players this way has a nonbiomechanical benefit as well. Limiting a player's choices improves his or her reaction time. The fewer the choices, the faster the reaction time.

When a defender must react to multiple possibilities, give the player an order of priorities for response. For example, tell the player, "Dig the line shot; if it does not come, dive for the dink." If the player is given the priority order, the reaction time to the primary stimulus is faster than in an equal-choice reaction time.

Rule Two: Attain the optimum biomechanical position for the expected movement responsibility.

The ability to apply maximum force for movement in a given direction depends on several factors, including the following:

- The number of muscles involved: The greater the number of muscles involved, the higher the probability for a large force.

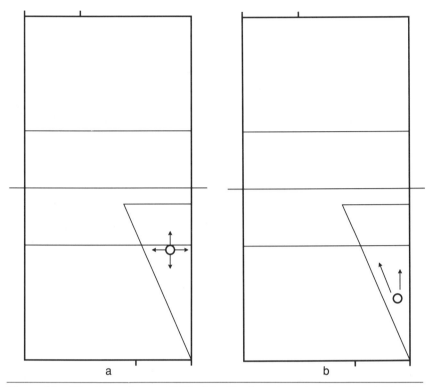

Figure 3.1   Directions of responsibility (a) with player in center of zone and (b) with player in rear of zone.

- The combined power generated by those muscles at the joint angles used: Large muscles generate greater forces than smaller muscles, and forces exerted by muscles vary throughout the joint angle.
- The percentage of the force applied that propels the center of gravity of the body in the desired direction.

It's best to have powerful muscles push through the body's center of gravity in the desired direction.

The center of gravity of the ready body is not far from the belt buckle, or the player's navel. If the player is to move horizontally, the forces applied by the legs must be behind the center of gravity. If the player is to jump, the legs must be under the player.

In Figure 3.2a, the sprinter's legs are behind the center of gravity, allowing effective movement forward. In Figure 3.2b, the tennis player's feet are wide, positioning the player to move equally well to either side but not allowing easy forward movement. In Figure 3.2c, the volleyball serve receiver has a foot position similar to that of the tennis receiver and should be able to move sideways easily, but not forward.

Figure 3.2 (a) Sprinter with driving force behind center of gravity, one-directional movement; (b) tennis player with wide stance, two-directional movement; (c) volley-ball player with wide stance, two-directional movement.

In Figure 3.3, the volleyball serve receiver has a wide and staggered foot position with right foot forward and left foot back. This allows the player to move fairly well to either side and is a good position for moving forward in the direction of the right foot. However, it would be unreasonable to expect this player to move forward and to the left efficiently.

Complicating this biomechanical discussion is the fact that many players are one-footed. They tend to move the same foot first, no matter what the biomechanical situation or disadvantage; they cannot efficiently move the other foot first. Our suggestion is, try to train the other foot. If this

Figure 3.3 Volleyball player with wide and staggered foot position, four-directional movement.

is not possible, align the player's body so that he or she can move fairly well in the desired position.

In the wide and staggered, one-foot-forward position (Figure 3.3), the player can retreat backward in the direction of the left foot, but this movement is not efficient. Because of the nature of the spine, hips, knees, and ankles, forward movement is more efficient than backward movement.

Another complication with backward movement is that after the player moves backward, he or she must then reverse that movement to move or swing forward into the ball. This reversal is extremely difficult, both physically and mentally.

Rule Three: Eliminate false steps.

For a number of reasons, many players use false steps in their normal movement patterns. False steps are steps that are not in the direction of the desired movement. For instance, it is common for a blocker (Figure 3.4a) to move the left foot to the left (Figure 3.4b) before stepping to the right to block (Figure 3.4c).

False steps have three common causes. As mentioned previously, many athletes always move the same foot, regardless of movement pattern or direction. Often training will reduce this false stepping. Another reason athletes use the false step is to position the pushing foot far enough away from the center of gravity to make the push effective. In this case, the

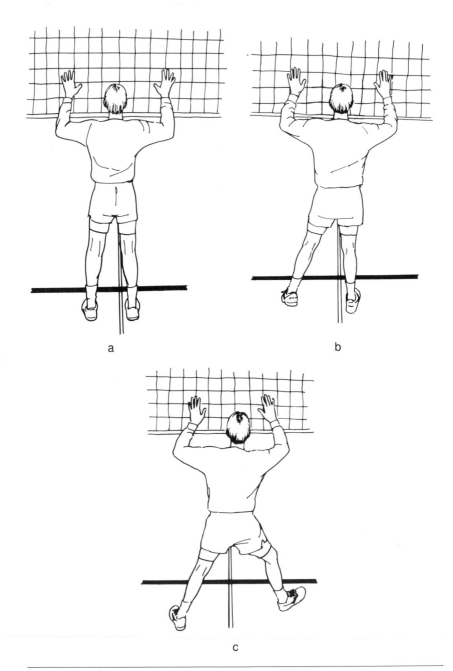

Figure 3.4 Blocker (a) ready to move, (b) moving with false step to left, and (c) moving to right after false step.

feet should probably be wider in the initial position, and you should evaluate the athlete's starting position.

The third reason that athletes use false steps is to achieve a springlike return of energy by quickly loading the pushing foot. This action increases the force with which the athlete can push off and increases the speed of subsequent movement. However, because of the time the false step takes, the time for the total movement may increase. There have been no studies to resolve this problem.

Biomechanical Considerations of Blocking

Probably less is known about blocking than about any other phase of volleyball. Blocking, often the last skill to be perfected, is probably the most complex volleyball skill. Blocking, like spiking, is a primary determinant of which team wins.

The block has several functions:

- "Stuffing" the ball
- Deflecting the attack so that the blocker's team can control the ball for an effective attack
- Screening out an area of the court so that the diggers have greater opportunities for success
- Intimidating the opponent's attackers

Good blockers must be stable in the air. A blocker who drifts in the air may occasionally make a sensational block, but a stable blocker, in combination with a digger, is more likely to make successful plays.

Blocking success will also increase if the blocker can contact the ball before it reaches the plane of the net. Usually the blocker's initial contact with the ball is on the blocker's side of the net.

Here's a summary of the biomechanics of what a blocker must be able to do:

- Perceive where the setter will set and where the hitter will hit the ball
- Be ready to move left or right or to jump upward and to do the correct movement quickly
- Be high enough in the air to penetrate the opponent's air space and yet not hit the net
- Be stable enough in the air that the diggers have an opportunity to dig around the block

- Have enough spatial orientation so that a blocked ball will deflect in favor of the blocking team, either straight down into the opponent's court or softly upward on the blocker's side of the court
- Have enough strength and control so that the blocker can control the spike rather than the spike destroying the block
- Have the proper timing so that there is a possibility for success

Undoubtedly, an athlete's inherent abilities have a greater impact on blocking success than any other combination of factors. Repetitions of correct blocking techniques are necessary to train the movements.

Considerations for Initial Footwork

The blocker, especially the middle blocker, should be able to move equally well to the left and right and be able to jump quickly and effectively. In reality, this is nearly impossible.

Normally the blocker stands in the ready position as shown in Figure 3.5. Hands are high, toes are pointed forward, feet are fairly close together, knees are bent slightly.

Figure 3.5   Blocker in normal ready position.

The possibilities for movement from this position, however, are relatively poor. The knees are not bent enough to allow jumping quickly, and the feet are too close together to allow for efficient movement to either side.

Research (Coleman & Hannifan, 1976) tells us that each player has a specific optimum starting position. The feet are placed wider apart than in the position shown in Figure 3.5, and the toes are rotated outward. This new position (see Figure 3.6) allows both faster movement to the side and better jumping ability. Experiment with your players to determine the optimum foot placement for each.

Figure 3.6   Blocker in new, superior ready position.

The biomechanics involved are relatively simple. The wider base of the revised foot position applies a higher percentage of the driving force in the direction of movement. The rotated feet allow the plantar flexor muscles to apply driving force. This foot position also aligns the knee and hip extensors to apply driving force in the direction of movement.

The blocker's jumping ability is also improved in this ''pseudo-plié'' position. The hip adductor muscles are engaged and contribute to the jump, and the jumping forces are applied directly upward. In the more traditional jumping position, the hips are flexed and the center of gravity wobbles back and forth as the blocker jumps, resulting in a slower and less efficient jump and possibly less body control.

A problem related to body control in a block jump is that of the upper body movement during the jumping and blocking action. Commonly, especially in the normal jump, the upper body begins relatively close to the net. As the hips drive up and forward, the upper body and the arms drive backward. Near the peak of the jump, the arms must be placed over the net, but the only way to get them there is to swing them forward. Although this swinging action leads to some sensational blocks, more often it leads to loss of control and poor blocking.

If the blocker is expected to move from the initial position, definite footwork patterns need to be established. Many footwork patterns have been advocated by various coaches, but not enough data have been collected to determine the appropriate pattern in any given situation. A few general guidelines, though, need to be considered as various patterns are proposed. Among them are these:

- Each step costs the blocker time, so the number of steps should be minimized. On the other hand, lunging and overstriding are inefficient.
- The proposed footwork pattern should allow the blocker to arrive at the appropriate position and to jump without drifting sideways.
- A pattern that requires the blocker to rotate toward the net while in the air should be discouraged. Although a few players are successful with this technique, very few improve their blocking by using it.

Another problem related to blocking mechanics involves both movement and jumping patterns. If the blocker has only one or two possible attackers, the mechanical patterns are easily programmed and can be executed well. But today's typical blocker must keep track of at least three attackers, and one will be threatening a quick attack. Often this threat is such a dominant stimulus for the blocker that the mechanics of the block are affected.

Not only does the extra choice concerning the quick hitter slow the thought process and reaction time of the blocker, it often destroys the well-established movement program. Extensive training with multiple-stimuli will improve, but may not perfect, the blocker's response.

A simple drill such as one middle blocker practicing footwork against three hitters during warm-up will give the middle blockers practice. You need to give the blocker feedback on the mechanics of footwork during the drill.

Coaches often want blockers to do sideward movements that may be impossible to perform—certainly an unfair expectation. For example, the middle blocker may be expected to move to the outside to join with a teammate to block an outside set.

If the setter sets a quick set to the outside spiker, it takes approximately 1.3 seconds for the ball to reach the spiker. However, it takes an experienced, mobile middle blocker about 1.6 seconds to move to the ball and jump to block it. Add to this fact the reaction time delay caused by a potential middle attacker and the confusion caused by the movement of a potential outside blocker to the ball, and the middle blocker has little chance to get to the block effectively.

To help blockers solve their movement problems, in recent years many coaches have advocated a mechanical pattern that certainly has not been proven effective in the scientific sense: ''weight-loading'' a specific leg of the blocker (see Figure 3.7). In this technique the blocker, in the initial ready position, shifts more weight to one leg than the other. A number

Figure 3.7 Blocker in weight-loaded position.

of explanations are given for this, and some, but not all, may be accurate. Among the justifications for weight-loading are these:

- To move most quickly in the direction of the weighted leg
- To move most quickly in the direction opposite the weighted leg (obviously these two explanations are contrary)
- To allow the free leg to be the first one to move, no matter what the direction of movement. If the movement is in the direction of the free leg, then a ''jab'' with the free leg is used as the first step. If the movement is in the direction of the weighted leg, then the free leg crosses over the weighted leg on the first step.

From a biomechanical viewpoint, it seems unlikely that this technique can improve the blocker's ability to move along the net. Although no studies have addressed the technique, we believe that weight-loading inhibits the blocker's movement and jumping ability.

Considerations for Hand and Arm Position

No scientific evidence is available on the optimum hand and arm movements, but some guidelines appear to be defensible. Among them are these:

- Relatively high hand position in the ready position
- Elevation of the scapulae (shoulder blades) while blocking
- Elimination of the arm swing
- Hand position that surrounds the ball
- Contact with the ball on the other side of the net

Relatively High Hand Position in the Ready Position. The high hand position has been defined differently by prominent coaches. The 1984 USA Men's Olympic Team, which won a gold medal in Los Angeles, was trained to lock the hands and arms at maximum height (Figure 3.8). In this position, the wrists, elbows, and shoulders are fixed in a rigid position so that the blocker can touch any ball set near the blocker without having to move the hands and arms appreciably. This position keeps the arms out of the propelling phase of the jump. Because many blockers hit the net with their arms while jumping, this would seem to be a good compromise. The lack of arm swing sacrifices a small portion of the potential jump but allows fewer jumping errors and more controlled touches of the ball.

Most coaches have the blocker's hands begin in a lower position, near the height of the top of the head. Carl McGown, professor of motor learning at Brigham Young University, points out that the slow movements

Figure 3.8 Blocker in ready position with hands, wrists, and elbows locked.

in blocking occur in the legs. The hands and arms have relatively fast movement and can be held in a lower position (Figure 3.9) from which the arms can aid in body movement as the blocker moves along the net.

It is generally agreed that the blocker's hands should not be below the shoulders while the blocker is in the ready position and that the arms should not be used in the propulsion phase of jumping. The problems related to the arms being near or contacting the net or other blockers seem to outweigh the benefits of a small gain in jumping height.

Elevation of the Scapulae While Blocking.   Scapular elevation is a simple shoulder shrug. With training, players can learn to elevate the shoulders 1 to 4 inches above the normal shoulder position (Figures 3.10, a and b). If the athlete is both trained and strengthened properly, this elevation can be added to the height attained while blocking. The coach should give the blocker feedback on shoulder elevation.

Figure 3.9   Blocker in ready position with hands lowered.

Figure 3.10   Blocker with scapulae (a) in normal position and (b) in elevated position.

Elimination of the Arm Swing.   Many blockers tend to swing their arms while in the air. Among the reasons for this are the following:

- The arms are too far away from the net because of upper body movement while jumping.
- The blocker has learned the techniques of rotating the body in the air while blocking.
- The blocker is not strong enough to withstand the power of the spiked ball from a semistatic arm position.
- The blocker visualizes that this action is necessary to stuff the ball onto the opponent's court.

The lack of control, the tendency to hit the net, and the difficult job of playing defense behind a swinging blocker make the swinging block a low-percentage block. The coach should discourage athletes from using this block.

Hand Position That Surrounds the Ball.   Most blockers block with hands close together and the fingers pointing up (Figure 3.11). It would be better to widen the distance between the hands to at least one ball's width apart.

Figure 3.11   Blocker with normal hand position and spacing.

No studies have been done on the blocker's hand position, but the wider position would seem to allow the hands to rotate into a position to optimize blocking ability (Figure 3.12). In this position, the hands are rotated outwardly (thumbs are pointed upward), and the player is reminded of the appropriate hand position by stating "Surround the ball."

Figure 3.12   Rotation and wider spacing of blocker's hands.

The wrist position depends on the goal of the block. Usually the wrist should be flexed (bent forward) so that the ball will rebound onto the opponent's floor. At other times, such as when the spiker is tall or the blocker is short, the blocker may attempt a soft or defensive block. In this case the wrists are extended (bent backward) so that the ball will rebound into the air of the blocker's team.

Contact With the Ball On the Other Side of the Net.   Many blockers inaccurately think they block on the opponent's side of the net. In fact, most blockers actually contact the ball after the ball has penetrated the plane of the net. After contact, often the blocker follows through on the other side of the net. Blocking effectiveness improves by a factor of two to three when blocking contact occurs on the opponent's side of the net.

Here's an effective drill to help the blocker. A coach stands on a platform and spikes the ball into a block. A second coach, or a player acting as a coach, stands on the spiker's side of the net and gives the blocker feedback about the position of contact with the ball relative to the plane of the net.

Biomechanical Considerations for Spiking

The biomechanical aspects of the spike are numerous, and we will discuss just a few easily identifiable parts. Most of the concepts mentioned here follow sound biomechanical principles but have not been studied scientifically.

At one time or another, you've probably been impressed with the velocity of a particular spike. Most high-velocity spikes occur as players are warming up and are much more difficult to execute during competition, when net fault and blockers become influential factors.

The greatest difference between top international volleyball and the game that most of us teach is the velocity of the players as they are playing. At the top level, players hurl themselves around the court at sprint velocities. These players use techniques in which the momentum created by these high velocities is transferred to the ball during the attack.

The momentum, thus velocity, imparted to the ball is generated by many factors, including the following:

- The linear velocity of the spiker in the direction of the spike
- The spiker's torso rotation
- The spiker's arm velocity
- The velocity of the spiker's wrist snap
- The falling velocity of the spiker (the amount of drop of the spiker before the ball is contacted)
- The mass of the spiker's hand
- The rigidity of the spiker's hand
- The percentage of the spiker's force applied through the center of the ball

These factors can be summarized for the most part as follows: The spiker wants to apply force through or near the center of the ball with a high arm velocity and a violent wrist snap. A large, strong, stable, and massive hand increases the probability of high-velocity spikes.

Many hard spikers hit the ball on the descending part of the jump. Most coaches would prefer that the attack take place at a higher point and would sacrifice the small gain in ball velocity achieved by the increased downward velocity.

Probably the most misunderstood part of the spike is that related to the linear velocity of the spiker. In the traditional spiking technique, the spiker jumps from and lands at the same place on the court. This technique has some sound bases. There is less risk of missing the ball and little chance that the spiker will jump into or under the net. Using this technique, the spiker has no linear velocity and, in fact, is often falling or rotating backward as the ball is contacted.

In contrast, most hard spikers move with a high velocity in the direction of the attack. The spiker has a fast approach and large broad jump while attacking the ball. A broad jump of 3 to 5 feet is not uncommon. Part of the momentum created in this approach is converted to upward momentum to aid in the height of the jump. If the body is allowed to maintain some forward momentum, part of that can be transferred to the ball.

The broad jump allows for a larger zone in the air within which the ball may be contacted than does the stationary spike. If the spiker's approach is perpendicular to the set, a broad jump increases the depth of the hitting zone. Thus, the set need not be quite as accurate.

The broad jump also requires the set to be farther from the net than for the stationary spike. Some spikers think this is an advantage because the ball can be controlled around the blockers, whereas others think it is a disadvantage because the ball is too far from the block to be hit over the block.

Recently an old spiking technique has become popular again. This technique, called the *slide*, is commonly, but not necessarily, hit using a one-foot takeoff (Figure 3.13). The slide is unique because its approach is essentially parallel to the net and the set, whereas the normal spike's approach is approximately perpendicular to the net and the set.

If the set and the approach are in opposite directions, as in the traditional techniques, there is a relatively small contact zone, which yields little advantage. If, on the other hand, the set and the approach are in the same direction, the contact zone is considerably larger than a normal contact zone—a great advantage. Also, the spiker is flying past the relatively stationary blockers, thus spikers using the slide are experiencing a great deal of success.

Proper footwork during the approach also aids in the spiker's ability to hit the ball with high velocity. In most attacks other than the slide the spiker jumps from two feet. At takeoff, the spiker's hitting hip should be farther from the net than the nonhitting hip. This positioning is relatively natural for a right-handed spiker attacking from the left side of the court or for a left-handed spiker from the right side of the court. A right-handed spiker attacking from the right side of the court is shown in Figure 3.14a. Such a position allows the spiker to generate considerable rotational

Figure 3.13   Spiker's one-foot takeoff for slide.

momentum that may be transferred to the ball. An effective transfer takes place if the torso is stopped from rotating as the arm begins its forward swing and a whipping action involving the arm and wrist results.

Often a right-handed spiker attacking from the right side of the court rotates the hips before takeoff in order to see the set more easily. This loss of rotational momentum and relatively strange body position places the attacker in a poor biomechanical situation. The attacker using this backward body position on takeoff, from any position on the court, is called "goofy-footed" (Figure 3.14b).

The goofy foot position results because the right-handed spiker, learning to hit from the left side of the court, learns to face the setter who is in the middle of the court. This position forces the right hip to be away from the net as the spiker starts an approach—a biomechanically sound position. However, when the spiker is on the right side of the court, the comfortable position of facing the setter forces the right hip toward the net into a biomechanically inferior position.

Spikers may choose from a variety of approach angles. The player using the slide approaches almost parallel to the net. Although right-handed spikers using the slide normally move from left to right on the court, many players have mastered the slide in the opposite direction.

Approach angles are an individual matter, often influenced by team and coach preferences. Usually a right-handed spiker on the left side of

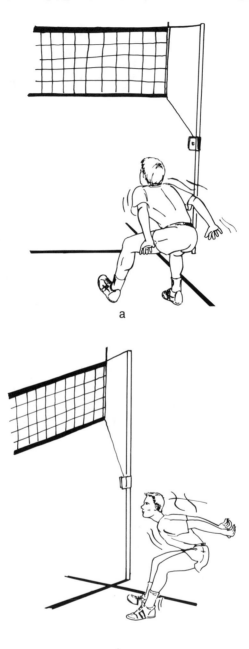

a

b

Figure 3.14 Spiker with (a) normal foot position and (b) goofy foot position on takeoff.

the court approaches at a 45-degree angle to the net. From the middle the approach angle is close to 90 degrees. From the right side of the court the approach is also close to 90 degrees, but the players generally move slightly toward the center of the net (Figure 3.15).

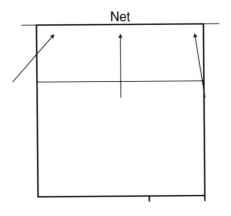

Figure 3.15   Spiker's approach angles from various court positions.

It is important for the young spiker to learn a correct and consistent footwork pattern. Coaches differ on the number of steps a spiker should use. The situation and distance from the net also influence the optimum number of steps. In general, only the final two steps determine the correctness of the approach pattern.

We will discuss the footwork pattern for the right-handed spiker (the pattern is similar, but reversed, for the left-handed spiker). A normalsized player takes from zero to two steps behind the 3-meter line, ending with the left foot on the 3-meter line. Then the spiker takes one large step with the right foot followed by a close step with the left. This should place the left foot slightly ahead of the right with both feet pointing in the direction of the approach (Figure 3.16). The jump will occur from both feet approximately 5 feet from the net.

The jump landing should be soft and within a foot or two of the net. Research has shown (Coleman & Adrian, 1984) that athletes who land softly have fewer back and knee injuries than those who land with greater force. The soft landing is on two feet; the athlete should cushion the landing with a controlled knee bend while maintaining a straight back.

Volleyball coaches disagree about the left foot position just before the jump takeoff. Many coaches believe that the left foot should be rotated

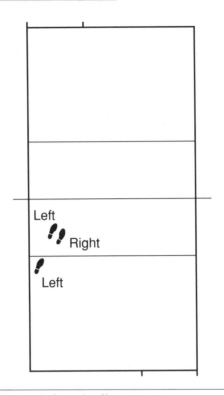

Figure 3.16   Spiker's steps before takeoff.

inward (Figure 3.17) so that the foot, at takeoff, is almost parallel to the net. Two reasons are given for this distorted foot position: It assures that the right hip is back on takeoff, and it inhibits the broad jump. We believe that neither of these reasons is appropriate for biomechanically good spiking technique. This distorted position probably stresses the twisted knee and the spiker's back, inviting injuries to both.

The coach should observe the spiker from behind and at the point of contact with the ball should be able to see a line of force. (This is not a true line of force in a biomechanical sense, because there is no base of support from which the force can be applied. The line represents an alignment of body segments, and the term is chosen here because of common usage.) The line of force for a right-handed spiker should be from the point of contact between the hand and ball, down the spiker's arm, through the center of gravity, and down the left leg of the spiker. This line should be vertical (Figure 3.18a).

A spiker who attacks the ball in this manner has a greater potential for high ball velocity, ball control, and maximum contact height. Distortions from the line may diminish both power and control and contribute to

Figure 3.17 Inward rotation of spiker's left foot.

a   b

Figure 3.18 (a) Line of force for right-handed spiker; (b) spiker contacts ball outside shoulder.

shoulder injuries. For example, the common technique of hitting the ball with the hand to the outside of the shoulder (Figure 3.18b) increases the strain on the relatively weak, injury-prone muscles of the rotator cuff and decreases the force with which the ball can be hit. The advantage of the quicker arm swing that this technique offers is probably not worth the greatly increased risk of injury.

Biomechanical Considerations for the Serve

Serves may be classified in many ways: by arm action, by trajectory, by ball spin, or by any combination of these topics. No single combination has proven to be superior to others. The only measure of whether a serve is appropriate or effective is whether it leads to the serving team scoring points.

The arm action for the serve may be classified in three general categories: underhand, sidearm roundhouse, and overhand. Most advanced players use the overhand serve.

Trajectories may be low to the net or high. They may also be short, served from the back line of the court, or longer, served from some distance behind the court. The short, low serve is common because the ball reaches the passer rapidly. On the other hand, many top players serve from great distances behind the court; commonly this is also a high serve. This serve has a high velocity in both the horizontal and vertical directions and often causes passers great problems.

Control of the spin of the serve is often baffling to the beginner. If force is applied through the center of the ball, the ball will have no spin as it travels through the air. A ball with no spin gathers irregular pockets of high and low pressure around it and responds to these pressure differentials by moving in an erratic pathway. This *floating* serve is the most common type used in high levels of volleyball. It is contacted with the hard part of the hand, either the heel of the hand or the knuckles.

If force is applied in a direction that is not through the center of the ball, the ball will spin. The spin may be applied in the direction of movement of the ball (topspin), in the direction opposite to the movement of the ball (backspin), or sideways (sidespin).

A spinning ball deviates from its normal parabolic pathway in a predictable manner. The topspin ball falls short of the expected target, the backspin ball travels long, and the sidespin ball deviates to the side in the direction of the spin. All serves, but especially spinning serves, become more difficult to control and to receive when there are air currents around the playing area. Thus, heating and air conditioning currents often affect the direction of movement of the serve. Outdoor air currents make it even more difficult to control the ball.

The chief disadvantage of the spinning serve is the control of its trajectory. A ball with only a little spin does not deviate from its normal path and is easy to play. A ball with a large amount of spin has a much higher velocity toward the target, and this velocity makes the ball difficult for both the server to control and the receiver to pass. Whether such a serve is effective depends on the players involved.

Whereas most serves are floaters, most spikes have topspin. A floating serve is fairly easy to place into the playing court, but the high velocities of the floating spike make it difficult for most attackers to control into the court. The floating spike is also nearly impossible for the defensive player to dig accurately.

Biomechanical Considerations for the Floor Defense

Coaches advocate different body positions for playing defense. Each position should be based on the player's expected function. There are two basic body positions.

The first position is one of mobility. If the defensive player is expected to be mobile, the body position should facilitate mobility in the directions expected. This is the common defensive role of the middle back player in men's volleyball. It may also be used by defensive players closer to the net who are playing against teams that do not hit the ball with high velocity.

The function and body position should be similar to that of a basketball player guarding an opponent. Feet are apart and positioned for mobility. The knees are slightly bent, and the player is flexed slightly at the waist. Arms should be relatively straight, possibly separated, and in front of the body (differing from the basketball player). From this position (Figure 3.19) the defensive player should be able to move within the defensive zone and bring the arms together quickly enough to control any ball hit into this zone.

The second position is one of imminent danger, in which the player may defend against a ball hit with high velocity right at the defender. This is the common role of the side defenders against a hard-hitting quick attack. From this position the defender should not be expected to cover a large defensive area. In this position (Figure 3.20) the player is in a low, wide-based, passing position with the feet staggered. The defender's

Figure 3.19   Defensive player in mobile position.

Figure 3.20   Defensive player in imminent danger position.

arms should be together or nearly together because there is not sufficient time to bring the arms together when defending against a high-velocity attack.

There also is a difference between the ready-for-defense position and the actual defensive position. The ready-for-defense position is the athlete's position as the ball approaches the opposing setter, and this position has two components: the exact position on the court and the expected body position.

For instance, consider the athlete playing defense on the left sideline against a team with a powerful three-hitter attack. In the ready-for-defense position, this player may be positioned within one foot of the left sideline, facing the opponent's middle attacker, in the imminent danger body position. If the ball is set quickly to the middle attacker, the defender is in position to defend against the fast attack. If the ball is set to the right side of the offensive court, right down the line from the defender, the defender should take one step backward and reassume the imminent danger position. If the ball is set to the left side of the offensive net, crosscourt from the defender, the defender should face the attack and assume the mobile defensive position.

Whatever the defensive position, at the moment of the attack, the defender should not be moving away from the net or from the attacker. It is especially difficult for the net players to move off of the net and then prepare to defend against an attack. For instance, a left front player may be expected to defend against a crosscourt attack from the opponent's left side. Often the defender moves away from the net and has his or her weight on the rear foot as the ball is being attacked. The correct position is to be shifting the weight toward the attacker as the ball is being hit. Similar considerations can be made for middle back players who are asked to move across the back row to dig line shots in certain defenses.

Considerations for Serve Reception

The ready position for the serve receiver is similar to the mobile defensive position. The receiver should face the server and be ready to move in the directions that are described by the coach as the most probable for a player in that position. At times these will be primarily sideways, and at other times they will be forward and back. Generally mobility in all directions is desired.

Considerations for Ball Contact on Defense or on Serve Reception

Ball contact is similar for both the digger and the serve receiver. In general, the passer's hands should be locked together so that the forearms form a platform. The platform is angled so that its flat surface is directed toward the setter. Many players make the mistake of attempting to direct the ball by swinging their arms parallel to the floor rather than directing the platform toward the target.

The passer's arms should be locked straight, long before the ball makes contact with the arms. The passer should attempt to be directly behind the ball at the time of contact (Figure 3.21a), because the ball is more easily directed to the setter from this position. Passing a ball from beside the passer is more difficult but acceptable. The main problem of passing the ball from the side is that it is more difficult to angle the platform (Figure 3.21b) for the precise contact necessary to direct the ball to the desired target.

Figure 3.21   Passer (a) behind the ball on contact and (b) beside the ball on contact.

We believe that passing accurately and consistently requires greater strength than most coaches realize. The stronger the passer, the less the amount of arm swing needed on ball contact. As arm swing is diminished, timing the pass becomes a smaller problem and the passer has a greater opportunity to be accurate. We think that minimal arm swing is desirable.

Biomechanical Considerations for Setting Footwork

We offer some simple observations to aid setters. There is little agreement among coaches and no research to support the opinions given here, yet the following concepts appear to have biomechanical support.

As the ball is passed, the setter stands about one arm's length from the net, to the right of the center of the net, and faces the left side of the court with the body opened up to the passer (Figure 3.22). Note the foot position with left foot trailing and the right foot aimed toward the left side target.

As the ball approaches the setter, the setter must make several technique choices. High-level setters jump set most of their sets. (We will not discuss jump sets except to encourage all who aspire to greatness to master this technique.) Most setters, with their feet on the floor, have much better ball control when they face the expected target exactly, or face exactly opposite to that direction when releasing the ball. All developing setters should learn to face the target when setting.

Figure 3.22 Setter awaiting a good pass near the net.

For setters who set with feet on the ground, coaches seem to advocate one of two footwork patterns: the parallel foot position (Figure 3.23a) and the staggered foot position (Figure 3.23b).

In the parallel foot position, the primary control of the direction of the set is the proprioceptive sense that both arms and hands can propel the ball with exactly the same force in the direction of the target. (Proprioception is reception and interpretation of the stimuli received from one's own muscles, joints, and tendons.) In the staggered foot position, the setter steps in the direction of the target, normally pushing from the left, trailing foot, onto the right, leading foot. The movement of the body, as it steps toward the target, contributes to the momentum of the ball in the direction of the target and, we believe, leads to more accurate setting.

For balls passed perfectly to the setter near the net, the difference in results between the two techniques may be slight. The major difference appears to occur when the ball is passed away from the net. When the ball is passed near the 3-meter line, the setter must move away from the net and be able to set the ball accurately, usually to the left front attacker.

With the parallel foot position, the setter moves away from the net, pivots on the right leg, and sets the ball as the left leg is brought into the parallel position facing the left front hitter. This often results in the set being made as the setter is pivoting on the right leg. With the staggered foot position, the pivot is made on the left leg as the right foot moves in

a   b

Figure 3.23   Setter in (a) parallel foot position and (b) staggered foot position.

the direction of the left front target. The staggered foot position appears to offer a better chance for an accurate set, because body movement at ball contact is linear in the direction of the target rather than angular.

Finally, the set should be made so that an observer in the profile position can see a line of force (Figure 3.24). This line of force should begin on the floor between the setter's feet, pass through the setter's center of gravity and along the setter's extended arms, and terminate in the direction of flight of the ball. The practice of falling backward while setting violates this principle and increases the difficulty of making a strong, accurate set.

PUTTING BIOMECHANICS TO WORK FOR YOU

The most powerful moderators of performance are feedback and repetition. When you ask athletes to modify biomechanical techniques, provide opportunities for them to receive both high numbers of repetitions and, at the same time, accurate feedback. In order for the athletes to receive these benefits, you must carefully plan practice sessions.

Suggestions for training include the following:

Figure 3.24   Setter's line of force.

• Decide what modifications are important to winning. For instance, a player may have poor defensive and poor serving techniques. The defensive flaw may cost the team only one rally per game, whereas the serving flaw may cost three rallies per game. It may be more beneficial to practice serving.

• Be certain that the changes you suggest are accurate and possible. For instance, you may believe that a spiker needs to jump higher. However, there is little evidence to indicate that a higher jump will aid a spiker, and probably little can be done in a short time to improve jumping.

• Designate some part of practice for working on technique. Often this is done soon after warm-up, early in the practice. Tell the athletes that the specific technique that was practiced will be emphasized or evaluated during the remainder of practice. Players should be encouraged to try different techniques as part of practice.

• Because players generally outnumber coaches, players should be trained to give each other specific feedback. For instance, the opening statement of this chapter required a coach to observe whether the blocker was making the initial steps in the correct direction. During drills, the next blocker can be the ''coach'' giving feedback. Then the athlete who has just given feedback will know exactly his or her expectations for the drill.

• Make sure your athletes watch performances of proper mechanics. It's best to have demonstrations done by fellow athletes who execute the various skills with mechanically correct techniques. A second choice is for a coach to demonstrate the correct technique. Make videotapes, films, photos, and posters available for the athletes to view the proper techniques. Mechanics can be discussed informally before, during, and after practices.

• Video cameras and monitors should be available daily for the curious athlete to view his or her performance.

KEYS TO SUCCESS

- **Make players aware that proper biomechanical techniques will make them better players.**
- **Be certain that the techniques you suggest are biomechanically accurate and physically possible.**
- **Create situations in which players help each other correct biomechanical problems.**
- **Create opportunities for numerous repetitions with accurate feedback.**
- **Videotape practices and games so that the athletes may observe their own performances.**

REFERENCES

Coleman, J.E., & Adrian, M. (1984). *Teaching the mechanics of jump landing*. Paper presented at the Olympic Sports Science Symposium, Eugene, OR.

Coleman, J.E., & Hannifan, J. (1976). *The relationship between foot position and movement of the center blocker in volleyball*. Unpublished master's thesis, George Williams College, Downers Grove, IL.

CHAPTER 4

Exercise Physiology: Proper Conditioning

G. Thomas Tait
The Pennsylvania State University

It's the fifth set of a long and grueling match. Your setter is still chasing down every pass and putting up hittable sets; the whole team is still concentrating and executing properly; your spikers and blockers are jumping almost as well as they did in set #1; and your middle blockers are still dominating the net. Fatigue is not going to rear its ugly head to spoil this team's play. These players have had proper physiological training. It's the proper application of physiological training principles that enables players and teams to take the skills and tactics they have learned and to actually perform them successfully throughout the course of a match.

WHY EXERCISE PHYSIOLOGY IS IMPORTANT

Physiology is the study of the functioning of the human organism. There can hardly be a science that is more important for the coach to know, understand, and be able to properly apply. In its fundamental sense, physiology involves the functioning of each major body system used in playing volleyball (e.g., skeletal muscles, cardiovascular system, respiratory system) and how those systems interrelate. In its applied sense, physiology addresses how exercise affects the functioning of body systems as well as how those systems impact performance. If a coach knows the basic concepts of exercise physiology and how to apply them to volleyball training, players will not only end up in "good shape"; they will also be able to physically play the game as well as they currently know how, while at the same time being less prone to fatigue-related injuries. As a bonus, they will be physically prepared to handle the next step up the volleyball ladder that the coach (or the opposition) demands.

It's the responsibility of the volleyball coach to put together the knowledge, skills, and insights gained over the years into a training program that enables athletes to realize and utilize their physiological potential to play their sport. The most successful coaches are able to intertwine the science and art of coaching as they apply the physiological concepts—and that's what this chapter is all about. I present the scientific concepts of physiology and look at some of the bases for applying those concepts in realistic situations. I also address various components of fitness, or conditioning: flexibility, agility, strength, power, speed, jumping ability, aerobic endurance, and anaerobic endurance.

EXERCISE PHYSIOLOGY CONCERNS IN VOLLEYBALL

For your players to be successful in competitive volleyball, they must be highly developed in several physical and physiological parameters. The muscles must be strong, flexible, explosive, well-coordinated, and capable of sustaining intermittent bouts of intense exercise for 2 to 3 hours. On top of that, they must be resilient enough to recover in time for the next match. To do all this, the muscles need help from the energy-supplying support systems of the body, from the mitochondria in the cells themselves to the cardiovascular and respiratory systems. The coach needs to know about physiology to assess the players' conditioning level and to design training sessions that optimize the players' physiological functioning.

What Are the Most Important Concepts to Know About Training?

The two concepts you must keep in mind as you go through this chapter are the stress-adaptation principle and the specificity of training concept. Although the two will be explained separately, they are closely linked and interdependent when put into practice.

The Stress-Adaptation Principle

By far the most important concept in applying physiology to volleyball training is the stress-adaptation (S-A) principle. Simply stated, if the human body is subjected to a stress, it in some way changes to adapt to it. No matter what component of fitness or conditioning you look at, the S-A principle applies.

Let's examine the terms *stress* and *adaptation*. Both are broad terms that can describe either a single type of stressor (e.g., stretch placed on a muscle) and its impact on a particular body part, or the collective influence of a complex series of stressors. In general, a *stress* is any stimulus, condition, or circumstance to which the body is subjected; the *adaptation* is what results if the stimulus is strong enough and repeated often enough to evoke a change.

If your training program is to properly apply the stress-adaptation principle so the desired outcomes develop, you must select and administer the correct stress so that the adaptation that most benefits players' physical abilities results. The training you provide for players is the stress, and the end result of the training is the adaptation. Because each aspect of a training program is a specific application of the general S-A principle, you must continually make right choices when developing various elements of training to produce players who are properly prepared for the rigorous demands of competitive volleyball. This chapter should help you make those choices wisely.

Specificity of Training

Now let's take a look at *specificity* of training. Almost every coach in every sport has learned that "training is specific." But it doesn't require any long-term, sophisticated research to discover that many volleyball coaches either forget the concept or don't know how to apply it. Training programs around the world are filled with examples of improper application of specificity of training. How else do we explain why coaches have players practice skills in ways that have no relationship to the game, or why they recommend that players wear weighted shoes to develop jumping ability? The concept of specificity in those instances somehow got lost.

The concept actually refines the S-A principle, addressing details like these: What kind of stress is needed? How much? How often? When and how should it be applied? Asking such questions is a way of searching for specific means to specific ends. In integrating stress adaptation and specificity as they are applied to a specific training regimen, you (the coach) must first know the exact demands that success in volleyball places on the players. You must then translate those demands into specific desired training outcomes. With those outcomes in mind, you select and apply the correct kind of training stress to the correct body systems with the correct intensity, duration, and frequency. The result? Progress in the right direction.

If, for example, you know blockers must develop a specific lateral movement endurance to be able to block effectively late in a match, their training must include many repetitions of that exact movement pattern under circumstances that mimic those of a game. Strength training won't do the job; nor will the typical "suicide" wind sprints (forward and back between various lines on the floor) that so many coaches jealously cling to because "We've always done them this way."

Where Does the Energy to Play Come From?

Athletes get the energy to play from the food they eat, especially carbohydrates and fats. But before the body can use the energy in food, the energy must be converted into another form; each cell converts the energy into high-energy molecules called ATP (adenosine triphosphate). ATP is the only immediate source of energy the cells can use to do work (e.g., contract muscle cells). In order for the muscles to use the ATP molecule's energy to contract, the ATP molecule must first be broken apart, releasing usable energy to do work. Then the ATP must be replenished or put back together. That resynthesis process requires energy from one of three sources; which source is used depends on how quickly the ATP must be replenished, and that depends on the intensity of the exercise.

The slowest source is also the most abundant. Most ATP is supplied through an aerobic, or oxygen (O_2) requiring, process within the mitochondria of each cell. Blood-supplied oxygen combines with simplified food sources (glucose, amino acids, fatty acids) and uses the energy from food to put together ATP molecules. Then the energy from the food can be used for muscular exercise. So the O_2-ATP system is a long, complex series of reactions that extracts energy from food and converts it into

ATP. Then the energy is readily available to be liberated by the breakdown of ATP and used to play volleyball. Although the system is relatively slow, it is virtually limitless so long as the blood can supply oxygen and food to the mitochondria, and the O_2-ATP system doesn't cause the rapid fatigue that characterizes the two faster systems. The basic overall reaction is Food + O_2 —> ATP + CO_2 + H_2O. (CO_2 is carbon dioxide; H_2O is water).

The two quickest sources of resynthesis energy are called anaerobic because they initially require no oxygen. The quickest comes from the breakdown of PC (phosphocreatine, another high-energy molecule in the cell that is similar to ATP); the other comes from the partial breakdown of glycogen (a process called anaerobic glycolysis). Although these sources are fast, they are limited in the amount of energy they can supply by their fatigue-producing by-products (e.g., lactic acid). These sources typically help resynthesize ATP during and immediately after very intense exercise. However, these sources are secondary, supplementary sources that kick in to supply needed resynthesis energy only when the primary aerobic energy source is too slow to meet the needs of the exercise.

To summarize, when a person exercises at slow to moderate intensity (e.g., during the general milling around that occurs between rallies), the O_2-ATP system can fairly easily resynthesize the ATP as it is broken down. However, during volleyball rallies, the jumping, sprinting, and other explosive movements require ATP breakdown and resynthesis at a faster rate than the aerobic system can supply; so the anaerobic glycolysis and/or PC systems supply the additional energy. Eventually (after the rally or during a pause) the aerobic system replenishes the depleted PC stores and helps eliminate (or use) the lactic acid that accrued during anaerobic glycolysis. Consequently, the O_2-ATP system is the primary energy source for the volleyball match.

Fortunately, the body's muscles and support systems (cardiovascular, respiratory, mitochondrial) are trainable, improvable, and adaptable. Properly designed workouts can help players maximize their physiological capacity.

What Is the Relationship Between Force and Time in Muscular Contractions?

The relationship between force and time is an important concept to keep in mind when you design workouts to develop strength or cardiovascular endurance. Every muscular contraction requires two factors: the contractile *force* generated and the *time*, or duration, of that force. When a player exerts maximum effort, force and time are inversely related. The closer the player comes to exerting maximum force, the less time (shorter duration, fewer number of repetitions) that force can be exerted. Conversely, when players need to exert effort for a long time or for many repetitions, they cannot exert a force that is near their maximum capability.

When applying the S-A principle to strength development or cardiovascular endurance development, consider the inverse relationship between force and time. Strength and cardiovascular endurance require opposite kinds of stress (training) for optimal results (adaptation). If you want players to get strong, emphasize contractile force and minimize the time (or reps) factor. And if endurance is what you're training players for, get them out of the weight room!

PUTTING EXERCISE PHYSIOLOGY TO WORK FOR YOU

Many of the concerns that surface during discussions among volleyball coaches are related either directly or indirectly to physiology. They are concerns such as these:

- *Strength training*. Just where does strength training fit into the overall picture, and what is the best way to train for strength? The answers to those two questions are both simple and complex.
- *Jump training*. Every coach wants to see his or her players jump higher maximally and continue to jump high late in a match or tounament. These are related but separate concerns, each of which can be improved through proper training.
- *Cardiovascular endurance training*. How do you do a good job of conditioning your team for tough five-set matches without taking away from the time they need to spend on other aspects of the game, like skill development? This is where the more modern approach to volleyball training methods has helped to revolutionize individual practice sessions.
- *Avoiding back pain*. Among volleyball players, lower back pain is a frequent complaint. A well-structured training program can be of considerable help in avoiding and alleviating back pain.
- *Combining physiology with other aspects of training*. Integrated training methods played an important role in the 1984 climb to the top of the world by the USA men's volleyball team, and it is now a staple in the training programs of almost all outstanding teams. We will take a look at how you can integrate physiological training with all the other facets of training into efficient, effective practices.

The remainder of this chapter focuses on the individual components of fitness that your training sessions can influence. Each component is briefly explained, and then the fundamental concepts and principles that should guide your thinking when setting up drills and practice sessions are explored.

What Is Involved in Strength Training?

Let's begin by defining three basic terms: strength, power, and muscular endurance (or strength endurance). *Strength* is the ability to exert contractile force in a single effort. *Power*, sometimes called explosive strength, is the rate at which force is applied; in other words,

$$\text{power} \quad = \quad \frac{\text{force} \times \text{distance}}{\text{time}} \quad = \quad \frac{\text{work}}{\text{time}}.$$

Muscular endurance (or strength endurance) is defined as the ability to either sustain or repeat a contraction over a period of time when that contraction involves a high percentage of the person's maximum strength. Strength, power, and muscular endurance are interrelated; you can't train for one without influencing the others. However, because of the specificity of training, we consider the three separately.

"Pure" Strength

Volleyball players need to develop strength for power or explosiveness, joint stability, muscular endurance, and injury prevention.

Maximum strength is determined by the force of the individual muscle fibers and by the number of fibers that can be recruited during any single contraction. Thus maximum strength depends on the protein infrastructure (i.e., the contractile filaments of the fibers) and the neuromuscular coordination required to exert force. Both factors can be improved through strength training by applying the S-A principle. Simply stated, the principle can be applied as follows: Make the muscles exert at least 75 percent of maximal contractile force every other day for at least 6 weeks; do each exercise for 1 to 3 sets of 1 to 12 maximum repetitions. These figures are only guidelines—not magic numbers that must be strictly adhered to.

If you follow these guidelines in designing a strength-training program, your players will develop strength regardless of the program specifics. Your program can be conducted in an expensive, fully equipped weight room or in a gym with no equipment (using self-resistive or partner exercises). You can use isometric, isotonic, concentric, eccentric, or isokinetic contractions, or any combination of these; strength will still be the outcome. But because of the specificity concept, it would be best to strength-train using isokinetic or concentric isotonic exercises through a full range of motion for each exercise. Those are the types of muscular actions used most often in volleyball.

Different Forms of Resistance Training	
Isometric:	Muscle length does not change, as in trying to lift an immovable object.
Isotonic:	Muscle length changes, but force applied remains constant, as in bench-pressing free weights.
Concentric:	Muscle shortens, as in curling a barbell up. Often called *positive work.*
Eccentric:	Muscle lengthens, as in slowly lowering a barbell after a curl. Often called *negative work.*
Isokinetic:	Speed of movement remains constant, but resistance accommodates to the force applied, as when using the Cybex Orthotron.

To further insure that strengthening exercises specifically apply to volleyball, choose exercises that imitate the movement patterns you want strengthened. Then add resistance so that the player must exert near-maximum force to perform the movement. For complex movements (e.g., the spike), train each component separately. That way, sufficient resistance is applied to all muscles involved.

For weak players who need to build basic strength, the kind of contraction used or the manner in which resistance is applied is not critical. Emphasize high resistance (or weight) and few repetitions (6 to 10). But encourage players to contract explosively on each repetition so they'll develop the explosive strength needed for volleyball (unless there is a danger of injury from a fast contraction).

Power

Explosive strength is vital for volleyball players. They need it to jump their highest, hit their hardest, get to balls that other players can't. As defined earlier, power has two major components, strength (force) and speed (time required to complete the movement). Players can increase their power output by improving in either component (or both). To develop power through strength training, the players should "explode" on every repetition, at least to the extent that the resistance will allow. Do not teach players to purposely lift slowly; have them train using slightly less resistance than they would use for pure strength development, and have them do 10 to 15 maximum repetitions.

An athlete's speed is largely determined by genetics. It can be improved at least somewhat through explosive strength training, through learning efficient movement techniques, and through speed training. Teach players efficient techniques to apply what explosive force they might inherently have in the right direction. Some players waste force by scattering it in different directions or even applying it in an opposite direction.

Speed training consists of performing the exercises at maximum speed with no added resistance or even below-normal resistance. For example, some sprinters and jumpers have developed faster leg speed (and thereby greater power) through downhill sprinting; the downhill slope causes the athlete to go faster and provides below-normal resistance. Volleyball players who gain strength through explosive resistance training and gain speed in the same movement through speed training should gain increased power in that particular action (i.e., greater force in less time).

Muscular Endurance

This is the kind of strength that good back-row defense demands. Muscular endurance in the legs enables players to maintain the low postures required and to make the constant readjustments needed on defense. Training for muscular endurance is fairly simple. Just decrease the resistance and increase the number of repetitions a little more than you would for power training. And don't forget specificity. Have players perform the movements or postures without the usual rests of coming back up to a high ready position, or have them initiate the basic defensive postures and movements with added weights (barbells, dumbbells, weighted belts), or have them do both. Most players have been doing exercises that develop muscular endurance (e.g., sit-ups and push-ups) for years. Once players are doing about 12 to 20 maximum repetitions, they are developing strength endurance.

What Is Involved in Jump Training?

Jumping ability is one of the most important abilities for volleyball players, so jump training is an important part of the physical training regimens of most successful programs. Jump training can increase the maximum vertical jump and improve anaerobic jumping endurance. The maximum vertical jump is more emphasized but perhaps less important and less successfully developed than jumping endurance. How high one jumps is determined primarily by genetics (i.e., the percentage of fast-twitch versus slow-twitch fibers in the jumping muscles). Maximum vertical jumping ability can be improved through explosive strength training. But it is more important to your team's success that players be able to jump nearly as high throughout a match as they can at the beginning. The setter needs to jump set potential overpasses in set #5 just as in #1, and blockers and attackers need to keep playing at the same height above the net as earlier in the match. Jumping endurance is a far more trainable trait than maximum jumping height. Training for one helps develop the other to some extent, but repetitions are the key to developing jumping endurance.

Another important factor in jump training that is often overlooked or underemphasized is form or technique, particularly arm swing. A mechanically efficient, powerful arm swing can help significantly in both maximum jumping height and in repetitive endurance jumping, and a proper foot plant is absolutely essential to jumping high. Apply the specificity concept to your jump training. Unless the jump training involves weights, machines, or something else that precludes ''normal'' jumping technique, insist that players use correct technique on every jump and that they jump many, many times throughout each practice. The more jump training is integrated with other training aspects, like skill development, the better.

Some jump training practices, such as depth jumps and some other forms of plyometrics (a bouncing type of exercise in which a concentric contraction is immediately preceded by a prestretch), elastic rope jumping, and jumping over objects or people, need to be reexamined relative to safety concerns, efficient use of practice time, and the specificity concept. After all, how many times in a match must players jump over something, down off of something, or up onto something?

Jumping ability is best trained through a combination of explosive strength training (with jumplike movements), drilling on correct jumping technique, and many repetitions of the jumps used in games.

What Is Involved in Endurance Training?

Volleyball requires both aerobic and anaerobic endurance. Anaerobic energy is needed when the ball is in play for explosive, quick movements. Between rallies aerobic energy is used. Because the two energy systems are interdependent, training for one almost always improves the other. All endurance training stresses the cardiovascular and respiratory systems, making them more efficient support systems for the ATP resynthesis needs of the body during exercise. The stroke volume of the heart (amount of blood pumped per beat) increases, maximum oxygen consumption increases, and the respiratory muscles increase their endurance capacity.

Even so, the localized adaptations made by the muscles trained and the difference between the aerobic and anaerobic energy systems makes endurance training very specific. Endurance training increases fuel storage (in the form of glycogen), blood supply, and mitochondrial activity in the trained muscles only. It also increases capacities for work that are unique to each of the three energy systems (PC, anaerobic glycolysis, and aerobic).

Because the adaptations are action-specific and muscle-specific, the manner in which an athlete endurance-trains for a specific court position is important. For instance, middle blockers who endurance-train their legs by doing straight-ahead repetitive sprints are likely to fatigue when the game requires them to move laterally and to do lots of stop-and-go running. They must endurance-train in a manner similar to the demands of the game.

Aerobic and anaerobic training require different approaches. The specific system or systems trained depends on the intensity of training. Slow, continuous work (lasting several minutes to hours) is handled by the aerobic O_2-ATP system and improves a player's aerobic capacity. But that player may not be able to handle the anaerobic stresses of competitive volleyball unless he or she trains at the intensity that the actual game requires.

Anaerobic training involves many repetitions of short, high-intensity actions that profoundly fatigue the muscles quickly (from seconds to perhaps 2 minutes). It is probably the most important physiological element in a volleyball training program. Players must do many high-intensity repetitions before you can expect them to perform explosively at the end of a long, tough match. Players need to be able to explode repetitively during a rally (the PC system allows this), work at a relatively high intensity throughout even a long rally (anaerobic glycolysis helps here), and recover quickly between rallies so they are ready for the next (the aerobic system takes the major responsibility here). Therefore, all three systems must be trained to handle even the heaviest demands of the sport.

In contrast to strength training, endurance training should de-emphasize the role of contractile force (resistance to movement) and instead emphasize duration and repetitions. And endurance training should be done daily instead of every other day, as is the case for strength training. Please note that aerobic endurance training and strength training are at opposite ends of the force-relative-to-time continuum. You cannot expect players to develop maximum strength and maximum aerobic capacity at the same time; endurance training tends to decrease the effectiveness of strength training. But that's OK. Volleyball players need endurance more than they need massive strength.

What Is Involved in Flexibility Training?

Flexibility, the range of movement in a joint or series of joints, can often be significantly increased through training. This is true whenever extension of a joint is limited by the surrounding soft tissues (i.e., muscle, tendon, connective tissue). The benefits of increased flexibility are in some ways obvious—a decreased tendency to pull or strain muscles or an increased ability to perform skills, techniques, or movements that would otherwise be impossible (e.g., an off-balance desperation defensive save). A good year-round flexibility program can also help alleviate or prevent chronic lower back pain, a common problem among volleyball players. Such pain often responds well to increased flexibility of the hamstrings and the extensor muscles of the lower spine, along with good abdominal strength.

The method for doing stretching exercises has been studied extensively. Experts agree that stretching should be preceded by a warm-up. Increasing the internal temperature of the muscles and surrounding tissues leads to easier stretching and less chance of injury from the stretching itself. The actual stretching should be slow, sustained, and static stretching in which the stretch is slowly taken to a "sticking" point and held there for several seconds. The slow stretch produces less than half the tension increase in the stretched muscle that the old-style ballistic (bouncing) stretching produces. Ballistic stretching causes a stretch-reflex contraction of the very muscle being stretched, which is contrary to the purpose of stretching.

What About the Training of Other Fitness Components?

Other fitness components include agility, balance, and neuromuscular coordination. These components are more related to specific volleyball skills and techniques than they are to physiology. But the training guidelines are the same: Train using drills that closely mimic the desired skill, and do so often enough that the stress stimulates a positive change.

How Do You Integrate Physiology Into Each Practice Session?

A few years ago volleyball coaches, like coaches in other sports, started to separate and compartmentalize the various aspects of training (e.g., endurance, skills, team tactics, psychology), treating each aspect as unrelated to the others. They either forgot or misunderstood the concept of specificity of training. Players are complete, whole human beings. They need to be trained in an integrated fashion that puts all aspects of the game together, because that's what the game demands of its players for success. As much as possible, integrate physiological training with skill training, psychological training, and so forth. With the exception of strength training, it is fairly easy to incorporate physical conditioning into the whole of volleyball training.

What Kinds of Drills Are Best?

Some recent advances in volleyball training, especially continuous drills and goal-oriented scoring systems, are especially useful in designing integrated training sessions.

Continuous Drills

Rallies in a continuous drill or scrimmage do not end as they would ordinarily (e.g., with a "kill" or a ball-handling error); instead they continue. At the point when the rally would normally end, the coach (from the sidelines) puts another ball into play. The coach's toss or hit should duplicate the previous situation, thus making any player who just caused the potentially terminal error repeat the skill until successful. How hard the players have to work to be successful in the rally will be determined by the coach's ball feeding.

The rally ends when a predetermined goal is reached, for instance, when both teams have successfully executed five pass-set-hit sequences during the rally or when a kill occurs after 3 minutes of continuous play. If the drill-ending goal chosen is challenging but realistic, and if the coach does a good job of feeding the ball to control the tempo and intensity of play, continuous drills can be physiologically (and psychologically) demanding and a great example of integrated training.

Goal-Oriented Scoring Systems

Adding a goal-oriented scoring system to a drill makes it more gamelike, resulting in more specific training outcomes. The plus/minus scoring system is an example. A player or team scores a +1 for each good result and a −1 for each bad result. That way, a player or team must continue to concentrate and to work hard throughout the drill to maintain positive scores and to reach the overall target goal (e.g., a score of +5).

Another example, the "wash" concept, is an excellent tool for integrating the sciences in this book with the art of coaching. Bill Neville introduced the wash drill into the training sessions of the USA men's Olympic team as they prepared for their 1984 gold medal assault. In a wash drill, the goal is for a player or team to win a predetermined number of successes *in a row*; the important part is the consecutive nature of the goal. The player or team starts out at zero successes; if they do not reach the goal number in succession (no matter how close they come), their successes up to that point are washed out and the score reverts back to zero. Obviously, the scrimmage or drill can become quite long and intense as players try to execute consistently well enough to reach the overall goal and not lose their earned points in a wash.

Here's a simple example of a six versus six wash scrimmage. The overall goal for each team is to rotate through all six rotations before the other team does. To rotate one position, the team must win two rallies in a row, one rally that begins with a serve and the other that begins with a coach-tossed free ball. If each team wins one of the rallies, it's a wash and neither team earns the right to rotate. The serve could alternate between the two teams or remain with one team throughout, depending on the purpose of the drill. If the two teams are evenly balanced and you want to ensure lots of washes with infrequent rotations, toss the free ball to whichever team loses the just-completed serve rally, thereby making it likely that the losers of the serve rally will win the free ball rally and create a wash.

With a creative imagination and the specificity concept firmly in mind, you can use the wash drill idea to design many solid training drills. They could be four versus six, three versus three, three versus six, or any other combination; they could be handicapped by setting a different goal for each team; and they could incorporate isolated skills (hitters vs. blockers) or the entire game (like the modified scrimmage explained in the previous paragraph). And don't be afraid to combine the continuous drill and wash drill ideas; they go together very well.

KEYS TO SUCCESS

- **Any physiological stress eventually results in an adaptation.**
- **The exact nature of an adaptation depends mostly on the specific stress and how it is applied.**

- To achieve the desired outcome, the stress applied must mimic the actual demands of the game to a considerable degree.
- It is your responsibility to correctly apply physiology.
- Fatigue-produced errors can be minimized through proper physical conditioning.
- To improve performance, players must train all three energy systems well, especially the anaerobic ones.
- To develop strength, players must exert 75 percent or more of their maximal contractile force every other day for 1 to 3 sets of between 1 and 12 repetitions.
- Players who use few reps and greater resistance tend to develop more pure strength; if players decrease resistance and work at higher reps (12 to 20), they develop more muscular (or strength) endurance.
- Strength training should be done explosively whenever possible.
- Power can be improved through explosive strength training and speed training.
- Strength-training exercises should, whenever feasible, mimic the volleyball movements to which the new strength will be applied.
- Jump training should involve explosive strength training, technique training, and jumping endurance training.
- It's more important that players maintain jumping ability late in a match than that they jump very high at the beginning. Jumping endurance is far more trainable than maximum jumping height.
- Endurance-training exercises should mimic the game itself.
- Flexibility can best be improved through static stretching exercises preceded by warm-up.
- Agility, balance, and coordination are so skill-specific that they should be trained by playing the game itself or through game-like drills.
- Physical and physiological conditioning, except for strength training, is best developed through training regimens that integrate conditioning with the other aspects of the game.
- Goal-oriented scoring systems and continuous drills should form the backbone of every practice session.

RESOURCES

Anderson, J.L. (Ed.) (1987). *The yearbook of sports medicine, 1987.* Chicago: Year Book Medical.

Anderson, J.L. (Ed.) (1988). *The yearbook of sports medicine, 1988.* Chicago: Year Book Medical.

Brooks, G., & Fahey, T. (1984). *Exercise physiology, human bioenergetics and its applications.* New York: Wiley.

Clarke, H.H. (Ed.) (1973, January). Toward a better understanding of muscular strength. *Physical Fitness Research Digest* (Series 3, No. 1, pp. 1-19). Washington, DC: President's Council on Physical Fitness and Sports.

Clarke, H.H. (Ed.) (1974, January). Development of muscular strength and endurance. *Physical Fitness Research Digest* (Series 4, No. 1, pp. 1-15). Washington, DC: President's Council on Physical Fitness and Sports.

deVries, H.A. (1986). *Physiology of exercise for physical education and athletics* (4th ed.). Dubuque, IA: Brown.

Fleck, S.J., & Kraemer, W.J. (1988). Resistance training: Physiological responses and adaptations (Part 2 and 4). *The Physician and Sportsmedicine,* **16**(4), 108-118.

Fox, E.L., Bowers, R.W., & Foss, M.L. (1988). *The physiological basis of physical education and athletics* (4th ed.). Philadelphia: Saunders.

Fox, E.L., Bowers, R.W., & Foss, M.L. (1993). *The physiological basis for exercise and sport* (5th ed.). Madison, WI: Brown & Benchmark.

Geltsman, L., Ayres, J., Pollock, M., & Jackson, A. (1978). The effects of circuit weight training on strength, cardiorespiratory function, and body composition of adult men. *Medicine and Science in Sports and Exercise,* **10**, 171-176.

Humphrey, D. (1988). Abdominal muscle strength and endurance. *The Physician and Sportsmedicine,* **16**(2), 201-202.

Jesse, J.P. (1989). Misuse of strength development programs in athletic training. *The Physician and Sportsmedicine,* **7**(10), 45-52.

Krotee, M.L., & Hatfield, F.C. (1979). *The theory and practice of physical activity.* Dubuque, IA: Kendall/Hunt.

McArdle, W.D., Katch, F.I., & Katch, V.L. (1986). *Exercise physiology: Energy, nutrition, and human performance* (2nd ed.). Philadelphia: Lea & Febiger.

Murphy, P. (1986). Warming up before stretching advised. *The Physician and Sportsmedicine,* **14**(3), 121.

Noble, B.J. (1986). *Physiology of exercise and sport.* St. Louis: Times-Mirror/Mosby.

Scientists talk about strength training. (1980, August). *Swimming Technique,* pp. 14-25.

Stamford, B. (1985). The difference between strength and power. *The Physician and Sportsmedicine,* **13**(7), 155.

Stegeman, J. (1981). *Exercise physiology: Physiologic bases of work and sport.* Chicago: Year Book Medical.

Structure and function of skeletal muscle: A round table discussion. (1977). *The Physician and Sportsmedicine, 5*(5), 34-45.

Wilmore, J.H., & Costill, D.L. (1988). *Training for sport and activity* (3rd ed.). Dubuque, IA: Brown.

CHAPTER 5

Sports Medicine: Managing Injuries

Jan Ochsenwald
Competitive Edge Health Services

It's the middle of volleyball season and three players are sidelined by injuries. Susan can't play because of knee tendinitis. She's had it for most of the season, and by now it has gotten so bad that she can't play effectively. Lisa is sitting on the sideline with an ice bag on her ankle. She came down from a block and sprained her ankle landing on another player's foot. Karla is one of the team's best outside hitters, but due to nagging shoulder tendinitis she's had to restrict her practice time so she can play in competition.

Scenes like this are all too common in sports, whatever the activity. When injuries occur, it is extremely hard to be patient and allow the proper rest that effective treatment requires. Practicing and competing are at the center of life for athletes, and they can feel devastated when injury takes them out of action. Nothing can guarantee the prevention of injuries, but you can take steps to give your team the best chance for an injury-free season. This chapter will help you understand how to prevent injuries, what to look for if they do occur, and how to treat them.

WHY SPORTS MEDICINE IS IMPORTANT

Sports medicine is a broad term for the health care of athletes of any age and at every level of participation. The three primary professionals who practice sports medicine are physicians, athletic trainers, and physical therapists. These professionals work both independently and cooperatively. There is typically close interaction among caregivers on a sports medicine team, with the common goal of returning an injured athlete to action as soon as possible. They work together to evaluate and diagnose injuries and carry out treatment and rehabilitation protocols. Unfortunately these professionals are not readily available on-site to high school coaches and athletes.

Having an athletic trainer on-site is the best solution for preventing, treating, and rehabilitating injuries, but because of schools' financial restrictions and a lack of educated and qualified individuals to fill such positions, health care for athletes must sometimes be assumed by the coach. Coaches are too often put in the position of deciding the severity of injuries, how to treat them, whether to make medical referrals, and when it's safe for athletes to return to play. In the absence of a sports medicine professional, the coach is the first to learn about an injury.

Due to liability concerns, coaches must stay within certain boundaries when evaluating and treating injured athletes. Everyone is covered by the ''Good Samaritan Rule,'' but overstepping that line and providing care that you're not trained to give should be done cautiously. That is why the coach should usually refer injured athletes to sports medicine professionals, who are qualified to evaluate the problem and recommend treatment and rehab programs. Sometimes the answer is as easy as resting for a day, but often much more is involved, including intense rehabilitation, medication, exercise, and therapeutic modalities.

Therapeutic modalities help create an optimum environment for healing while reducing pain and discomfort. Modalities include heat, cold, water, electricity, massage, and any mechanical means used to promote healing. Treatments should be determined and carried out by physicians, athletic trainers, physical therapists, or coaches who have had training in sports first aid.

SPORTS MEDICINE CONCERNS IN VOLLEYBALL

Medical concerns in volleyball include injury prevention, handling emergencies and acute injuries, managing overuse and chronic injuries, and developing treatment and rehabilitation programs. Once an injury occurs, the initial treatment and specific rehabilitation prescription are typically done by a sports medicine professional. The primary concern for the coach is injury prevention—the key to a healthy team, one without injury or illness. You give your team its best chance for success by developing and implementing a strong injury prevention program. Let's begin by discussing the role of general conditioning and conditioning specific to volleyball.

Injury Prevention and Conditioning for Volleyball Players

The most effective way to prevent injuries through conditioning is to give athletes a solid fitness base. Components of this base include players' psychological profiles, sound nutritional practices, cardiovascular training, flexibility training, and strength training.

Psychological Profiles

No two athletes are alike psychologically, nor can they be made to fit a specific mold. Trying to manage every personality on a team is not easy. Individual traits must be considered with regard to an athlete's response to injury, treatment routines, and rehab programs. It is possible to see an extreme variation in how different athletes respond to and accept being injured. Some think it's the end of the world and cannot deal with the situation rationally; others take it in stride. Of course, the severity of the injury directly affects the response. We would expect an athlete to respond differently to a sprained ankle, which may keep him or her out of action for a couple of weeks, than to torn knee ligaments that could sideline the player for a year. Also, an athlete's response to injury may affect his or her performance in the classroom; relationship with family, friends, and team members; and eating and sleeping habits.

Talk with your team about how individuals respond differently to injuries and discuss the psychological aspects of injury. Also tell the players what you expect from them both on and off the court, while they are unable to participate. Emphasize that an injured player needs to be physically and emotionally involved with the team. It is important for athletes to always feel part of the team, even when they cannot fully participate. Unless a physician says otherwise, do not allow athletes to miss practice because of injury. If possible, suggest restricted workouts that allow the athlete to keep in good physical condition. The activities the athlete can do depends on the injury. An athlete with a sprained ankle should be able to hit a ball against the wall, and should also be able to do stretching and flexibility exercises, sit-ups, ball-control skills such as setting, biking, exercises that use resistance tubing, and weight training. If the injury is to the upper extremity (hand, wrist, arm, and/or shoulder) the athlete could do total body stretching and flexibility exercises, biking, leg weights, sit-ups, ankle strengthening, walking, and weight training. (These are just suggestions and not intended to be exhaustive.)

Show concern for your athletes, their injuries, and their emotions, but don't overdo it. The best you can do is provide an environment that is conducive, both physically and emotionally, to healing.

Nutrition

Many athletes and coaches know nutrition is important, but they don't know how to develop an individual nutrition program. An athlete's energy requirements depend on individual traits like weight, height, age, and gender as well as on the type, intensity, frequency, and duration of the sport. Daily training can double or triple an athlete's energy needs over the nontraining requirements. Normally people eat when they're hungry, but with the intense emotional and physical stress of training and competition (and a lack of nutrition knowledge), many athletes don't consume enough calories and essential nutrients.

Diet directly affects athletic performance. Think of the body as a fine-tuned engine that performs fantastically on the best fuel available. The body's fuel comes from food, so why not provide the best fuel possible? Eating a nutritionally balanced diet enables the body to perform at its best (see chapter 6 for more information on nutrition).

Coaches, athletic trainers, and other health professionals play an important role in educating athletes on the strong relationship between nutrition and athletic performance. The athletes think of these people as role models. So if you talk about the importance of good nutrition but eat junk food on the sidelines, your actions contradict your words. To promote good eating habits, coaches must educate athletes about wise food choices, provide the athletes with opportunities to practice making wise food choices, and, most importantly, set a good example.

Training

A good training program for an athlete of any sport should include flexibility, cardiovascular, and strength training. These three components should be done not only during the season but, more importantly, during the off-season to prepare the athlete for the competitive season. During the season, training in these three areas provides athletes with the best chance of preventing injuries and also enables them to perform to the best of their abilities.

But the human body wasn't intended to go nonstop without rest and recovery. Even the best machines break down if not taken care of properly. Taking 1 or 2 days off per week lets the body recover, which helps reduce the chance of chronic injuries.

Flexibility Training. *Flexibility* is the range of movement of a joint or group of joints and is influenced by the bony structures, muscles, tendons, and ligaments. Studies have shown that increased flexibility tends to decrease injuries, and that increased flexibility contributes to better athletic performance.

In setting up a flexibility, or stretching, program, determine the athlete's comfortable range of motion for each joint, and set a goal to increase that range of motion in all directions. Good flexibility can be attained relatively quickly but is also lost quickly unless the athlete follows a regular stretching program.

Volleyball players need flexibility in the upper and lower body because of the extent of movements required for spiking, blocking, digging, and serving. Have your team do stretching exercises daily, after a short warm-up (i.e., easy jog four or five times around the gym). Stretching should be done as a team so the coach can supervise and make sure the athletes use correct techniques. Flexibility exercises should work the entire body to give the athlete fluid movement through the complete range of motion. Be sure to include the quadriceps, hamstrings, calf muscles, ankles, hips, shoulders, wrists, back, and abdominal muscles.

Remember, a good stretching program can help prevent injuries, including chronic or overuse injuries. For example, the shoulder is a common site for chronic injuries such as tendinitis. Figure 5.1 shows stretching exercises that guard against shoulder overuse injuries. To minimize chronic back injuries, have your athletes do the exercises shown in Figure 5.2.

It is imperative that no athlete stretch beyond his or her normal range of motion. Don't try to increase someone's arm-swing motion by over-stretching the shoulders, for this may cause laxity in the joint and can lead to further injuries. A naturally tight shoulder provides stability and protection from injuries. Flexibility differs from person to person. Don't try to change what is normal for a particular athlete.

Cardiovascular Training.   Athletes should build a cardiovascular training base during the off-season and maintain it during the season. Volleyball matches vary in intensity and duration, and athletes must be conditioned to go the distance. A well-conditioned athlete not only performs better but also may be less prone to chronic injuries. As athletes tire, their techniques become less correct, and they become more vulnerable to chronic overuse injuries. For example, incorrect arm-swing techniques may lead to shoulder tendinitis, and poor jumping techniques can cause patellar tendinitis in the knee.

Rotator cuff stretch 1

Lying with your shoulder on the edge of the table, bend your elbow at a 90-degree angle. Relax the arm and let the weight gently stretch your arm down.

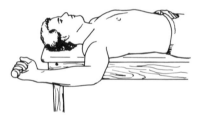

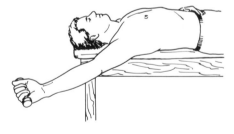

Rotator cuff stretch 2

Lie on the table with your shoulder on the edge of the table and your arm extended at approximately 135 degrees. Relax your arm and allow the weight to stretch your shoulder.

(continued)

Figure 5.1   Rotator cuff stretches.

Rotator cuff stretch 3

Lie on the table with your shoulder on the edge of the table, your head supported, and your arm extended straight back, behind your head, as far as is comfortable. Let the weight gently stretch your arm down.

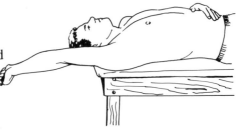

Posterior cuff stretch

In a standing position, keeping your body straight, gently pull your arm across your chest.

Inferior cuff stretch

In a standing position, lift one arm overhead. Put the arm behind your head and gently pull on the elbow with the other hand.

Figure 5.1   (*continued*)

Pelvic tilt

Lie on your back. Bend your knees, with your feet on the floor, and keep your arms at your sides. Now pull your abdominal muscles into a hollow position and push your lower back against the floor. The pelvis is being rotated downward. Hold for 6 seconds and relax slowly.

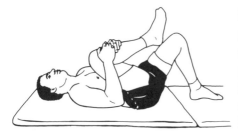

Knee to shoulder stretch

Begin in the same position as the pelvic tilt. With both hands, grab your right knee and pull it in the direction of your right shoulder. Repeat with your left leg.

Double knees stretch

Begin in the same position as the pelvic tilt. Grab both knees and pull them up toward the shoulders. Keep the back flat against the floor. Return the knees to the starting position and repeat.

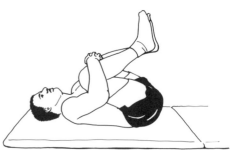

(continued)

Figure 5.2 Back stretches.

Back and abdominal stretch and strengthening

Get on your hands and knees. First relax your abdominal muscles, letting your back sag down. Then pull in those abdominal muscles, drop your head down, and round your back.

Trunk flexion in prone position

Get on your hands and knees. Tucking your chin into your chest, round your back; then slowly lower yourself until you're on your heels, with your shoulders lowered toward the floor. Your chest may be close to or resting on your thighs. Once in this position, relax 10 to 15 seconds. Then return to the hands and knees position while rounding your back and pulling in your abdominal muscles.

Figure 5.2 (*continued*)

The best cardiovascular training program includes both aerobic and anaerobic conditioning. During the off-season athletes should do endurance training (biking, running, stair stepping) for 30 minutes or longer three to four times per week; they should also do some type of sprint workout (running various short distances—60 to 400 yards—at three-quarter speed to full speed). During the season athletes need to maintain their endurance level, so after practice have them run laps in the gym, jump rope, or sprint.

Strength Training. Strength training should be done in cycles. The intense strength-building cycle is done in the off-season to maximize muscle strength. To do this, the athlete lifts heavy weights, which will probably cause muscle soreness (this is the reason this cycle is done during the off-season). The athlete does exercises that are specific to and simulate volleyball skills, along with general body strengthening exercises such as bench presses, bicep curls, and leg extensions.

During the season, the athlete should follow a maintenance strength cycle. The goal is to keep the strength gained during the off-season; maintaining muscle strength can result in optimal performance levels and reduce the incidence of chronic injuries. For example, knee tendinitis, specifically in the patellar tendon, is thought to be caused by weak quadricep muscles and the inability to have strong eccentric muscle contractions upon landing after jumping. The quadricep muscle is unable to stabilize the landing force, thus causing lots of force over the knee into the patellar tendon. This injury may be prevented by increasing quadricep muscle strength through knee extension exercises, other quadricep muscle exercises, and jumping. In addition, have your players do a few of the following exercises as part of the daily warm-up. The short time these exercises take is worth the time saved from possible injury time loss.

To strengthen any joint, one must strengthen the muscles that cross the joint. Two of the most commonly injured body areas for volleyball players are the shoulders and ankles.

To strengthen the ankle, work the muscles of the lower leg, which allow the ankle to invert (turn inward), evert (turn outward), plantarflex (foot pointed down, away from the body), and dorsiflex (foot pointed up, toward the body). An easy way to increase ankle strength is to exercise with surgical rubber tubing or wide rubber bands (1-1/2 to 2 inches), as shown in Figure 5.3. Have the team pair up and take turns doing each exercise for about 10 to 15 repetitions and 2 to 3 sets. The resistance varies by the distance the tubing is initially stretched and the width of the tubing. To strengthen the gastrocnemius (calf) muscle (used for plantar flexion), have the athletes do heel raises. These should be done on a step so the heel can drop below the step prior to each raise to increase the range of motion.

The shoulder sacrifices joint stability for joint mobility and is often affected by chronic injuries. The shoulder's range of motion allows for extreme movements. Many muscles cross the shoulder joint. The rotator cuff is made up of the supraspinatus, infraspinatus, subscapularis, and teres minor (see Figure 5.4). These deep muscles are the reinforcing, main stabilizers of the shoulder. The rotator cuff should be warmed up and stretched prior to the start of activity.

Ankle dorsiflexion

Start with the foot pointed down and pull the foot upward as far as possible. Then slowly lower the foot to the starting position.

Ankle inversion

Start with your foot in a relaxed position and pull your foot inward, with movement only at the ankle. Slowly bring your foot back to the starting position.

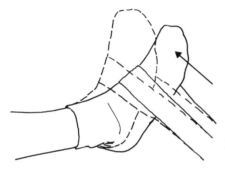

Ankle eversion

Start with your foot in a relaxed position and pull your foot outward, with movement only at the ankle. Slowly bring your foot back to the starting position.

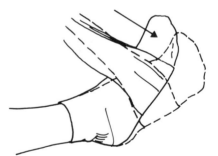

Figure 5.3 Ankle-strengthening exercises.

An excellent way to stretch and strengthen this joint is to use light weights (3 pounds—a tennis-ball can filled with sand is great) and do the exercises shown in Figures 5.1 and 5.5. Do 10 to 15 repetitions and 2 to 3 sets for each.

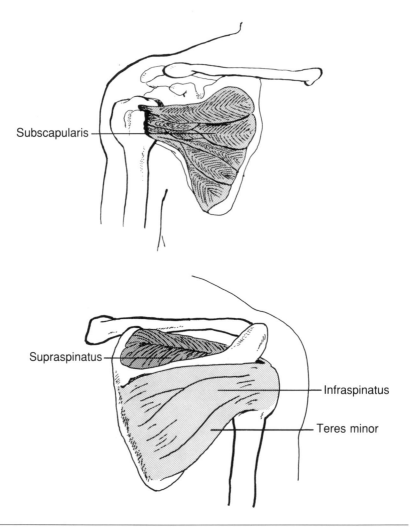

Figure 5.4 Rotator cuff muscles.
Note. From "Sports Medicine: Managing Injuries" by H. Amato. In *Science of Coaching Baseball* (p. 130) by J. Kindall (Ed.), 1992, Champaign, IL: Leisure Press. Copyright 1992 by Leisure Press. Reprinted by permission.

Supraspinatus strengthening

While standing, rest your hand against your leg, with your thumb midway between the front and side of your thigh. Slowly raise your arm. Keep your elbow straight and thumb pointed down. Lift your arm to just below the shoulder, then lower it slowly to where you started.

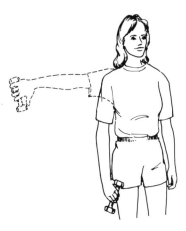

External rotation strengthening

Lie on your side. Keeping your elbow at your side, slowly lift the weight until your hand points upward. Then slowly return it to where you started.

Internal rotation strengthening

Lie on your back. Keep your upper arm against your side and extend your forearm out to the side. Lift the weight until your hand is pointed upward. Then slowly return it to where you started.

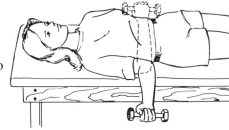

(continued)

Figure 5.5 Shoulder muscle-strengthening exercises.

Shoulder flexion strengthening

Stand with your arms at your sides. The thumb of the hand with the weight should be next to your thigh. Raise your arm in front of you and up into an extended position overhead. Keep your elbow straight as you move. As you lift your arm, rotate your arm so that when it is at the highest point, your thumb is pointed back. Return to the starting position. It's important to move slowly as you raise and lower the weight.

Shoulder abduction strengthening

Start with your arms at your sides. The thumb of the hand with the weight should be against your leg. Slowly lift your arm out to the side and up into an extended position overhead. As you lift your arm, rotate it so that when it is at the highest point, your thumb is pointed back. Return to the starting position. It's important to move slowly as you raise and lower the weight.

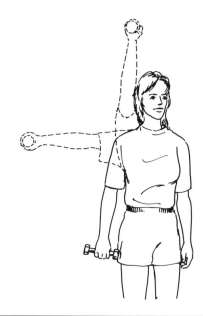

Figure 5.5 (*continued*)

Common Volleyball Injuries

There are two main types of injury: acute and chronic. An acute injury is characterized by rapid onset, a short course, and pronounced symptoms, such as a fractured finger, whereas a chronic injury is of long duration or recurs frequently, such as patellar tendinitis. Either type of injury can occur in any part of the body. Often the coach is the first to learn of an injury and must decide upon the appropriate course of action. In the following sections, injury evaluation, treatment, and rehabilitation are discussed, working from head to toe.

Facial Cuts

Although volleyball is a noncontact sport, sometimes a player collides with another player, or even with the floor. When this happens, the player may have a cut (laceration) on the chin (often from hitting the floor) or around the eye and forehead. Skin wounds of the face tend to bleed more than wounds elsewhere because the face has many blood vessels. If a cut occurs, stop the bleeding by applying compression to the area by using gauze and holding pressure with your fingers. Be sure to take the appropriate safety precautions when you're exposed to blood: Wear gloves to protect yourself from AIDS and other infectious diseases.

After the bleeding has stopped, cleanse the injury with antiseptic soap and water. You will need to determine the severity of the cut and whether stitches are needed. If the cut seems deep and the edges are far apart and/or in a place where butterfly bandages won't be sufficient, refer the athlete to a physician. If the cut is fairly small and the edges are smooth and not spread wide apart and deep, in most cases the wound can be closed with butterfly bandages. To apply butterfly bandages, apply a tape adherent around the cut, and then apply the bandages starting below the cut and pulling upward against gravity to ensure maximum closure (see Figure 5.6 for more complete instructions). Then apply a Band-Aid for further protection. If you have any doubts about whether the cut can be closed easily and securely with butterfly bandages, refer the athlete to a physician.

Concussion

A potentially more serious injury that a player could sustain is a contusion or bruise to the face or head accompanied by a concussion. A concussion is a syndrome involving an immediate and transient impairment in the ability of the brain to function properly. If an athlete receives a blow to the head, presume that he or she has received some degree of concussion. Most often the blow simply stuns the athlete, who recovers quite rapidly.

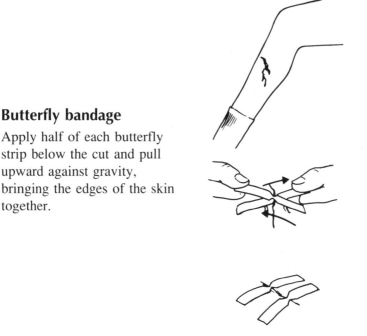

Butterfly bandage

Apply half of each butterfly
strip below the cut and pull
upward against gravity,
bringing the edges of the skin
together.

Figure 5.6   Butterfly wound closure.

To determine the extent of a head injury, you need to know the signs
and symptoms by which concussions are evaluated. Usually they are
graded I through III, with each grade having specific signs and symptoms.
A Grade I concussion, the most common type in sports, is minimal in
intensity. In general the athlete is dazed and disoriented but does not have
any loss of memory or consciousness; has mild or no dizziness and
headache; has mild or no tinnitus (ringing in the ears); and has slight or
no loss of balance. Allow the athlete a break from action or rest for the
time remaining.

A Grade II concussion is considered to be of moderate intensity, with
a short (5 minutes or less) or no loss of consciousness. Other signs and
symptoms are short-term or no loss of memory; minor mental confusion;
and moderate dizziness and headache, tinnitus, and loss of balance. Asking
the athlete simple questions such as "What day is it?" "What's the
score?" or "What school do you attend?" will help you determine the
severity of the concussion. Not being able to answer such questions quickly
and accurately is a sign of a more serious injury.

A Grade III concussion is caused by a blow of severe intensity and is
a serious medical problem. The signs and symptoms include loss of

consciousness for longer than 5 minutes; amnesia (inability to answer memory questions) lasting for a prolonged period; mental confusion; and severe dizziness and headache, tinnitus, and loss of balance.

To be safe, you should immediately initiate emergency care if the athlete exhibits signs and symptoms of a concussion more severe than Grade I. In such a case, have the athlete lie down and keep him or her warm and calm until help arrives. It is extremely important to never allow the athlete to return to any activity without the consent of a physician. Figure 5.7 summarizes the signs and symptoms of each grade of concussion.

Grade I: No loss of consciousness or memory; slight or no mental confusion; mild or no dizziness and headache; mild or no tinnitus; slight or no loss of balance

Grade II: No loss of consciousness or loss for 5 minutes or less; short-term or no loss of memory; minor mental confusion; moderate dizziness and headache, tinnitus, and loss of balance

Grade III: Loss of consciousness for more than 5 minutes; loss of memory for a prolonged duration; mental confusion; severe dizziness and headache, tinnitus, and loss of balance

Figure 5.7   Grades of concussion.

Shoulder Tendinitis

The volleyball player's shoulder is repeatedly put through three phases during the swing; cocking acceleration, follow-through, and deceleration. Repetitive throwing motions may result in tendinitis. Tendinitis has a gradual onset. Over time diffuse tenderness develops because of repeated microtraumas and degenerative changes (some tendon fibers are torn and become inflamed, causing pain and swelling—the first obvious signs of tendinitis).

If an athlete complains of pain during movement of the shoulder or any joint, you should suspect tendinitis. Review the techniques and biomechanics of the arm swing to rule out causes of the problem. Overuse of the shoulder muscles frequently affects the muscle and tendons of the rotator cuff (see Figure 5.4 for muscles of the rotator cuff), causing rotator cuff tendinitis. The principal rotator cuff tendon injured is that of the supraspinatus muscle. If the athlete feels pain when raising the arm from the side, this muscle and tendon may be inflamed. Table 5.1 shows movements that cause pain and their relation to the areas that may be affected. By having the athlete move the shoulder in these motions, you can better evaluate the muscle and tendon involved.

Table 5.1

Painful Motion and Possible Area Involved

Type of motion	Area involved
Passive lateral rotation	Joint capsule
Resistive lateral rotation	Infraspinatus
Resistive medial rotation	Subscapularis
Resistive elbow flexion	Biceps
Resistive elbow extension	Triceps
Resistive abduction	Supraspinatus

Note. From ''Sports Medicine: Managing Injuries'' by B. McAllister. In *Science of Coaching Swimming* (p. 113) by J. Leonard (Ed.), 1992, Champaign, IL: Leisure Press. Copyright 1992 by Leisure Press. Reprinted by permission.

If an athlete complains of pain, remove him or her from play and begin ice treatment. Apply an ice bag with an elastic bandage wrap over the injured area for 20 minutes, and have the athlete elevate the shoulder. Or give the athlete an ice massage using an ice cup. To use this treatment, you would previously have filled a paper cup with water and placed it in the freezer. To apply it, just tear down the paper until the ice is exposed, and rub the ice on the shoulder in a circular motion for 10 to 12 minutes. It's best to have someone else apply the ice so the athlete can elevate the shoulder to improve circulation.

If the athlete is not in pain and is able to participate in practice, either heat the shoulder with a heat pack for 20 minutes or use ice massage, whichever the athlete prefers. This treatment should be done before practice, followed by stretching exercises.

Monitor the athlete's activities. If he or she is unable to fully participate, modify the activities by decreasing the number and/or speed of arm swings, blocking attempts, and serves. If the athlete's shoulder is just too sore to continue to play, refer him or her to a sports medicine physician. If the physician recommends rest for the injured shoulder, have the athlete continue to do exercises that don't involve the shoulder, such as running, sit-ups, biking, or step-ups. That way, when the shoulder is ready to return to activity, so is the rest of the body.

Shoulder Dislocation

Shoulder dislocations happen primarily when forces cause the joint to go beyond its normal anatomical limits. Its wide range of possible movements makes the shoulder joint highly susceptible to dislocation. In fact, dislocation of the shoulder is second only to finger dislocations in incidence in sports. The most common kind of shoulder displacement occurs anteriorly (Figure 5.8), and it is usually the result of direct trauma. This type of dislocation is often caused when the arm is in a position of external rotation and abduction, as shown in Figure 5.8. The athlete with an anterior dislocation has the following symptoms: a flattened deltoid contour, deformity of the shoulder, loss of motion, severe acute pain, and possible numbness or tingling in fingers. Also, the athlete carries that arm in slight abduction and external rotation, doesn't want to move the arm freely, and describes feeling the shoulder slip out.

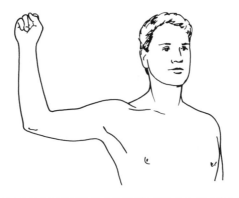

Figure 5.8   Common position that may cause shoulder dislocation.

A shoulder dislocation requires immediate reduction (replacement back into a normal position) by a physician; emergency procedures should be initiated. Try to keep the athlete calm, apply an ice pack, immobilize the injured arm with an arm sling or wrap the arm to the body with an elastic bandage wrap, and transport the athlete to a hospital or other medical facility.

Sports medicine professionals should treat the injury and supervise rehabilitation. Generally, after the dislocation has been reduced, the shoulder is immobilized for about 3 weeks. During this time the athlete does isometric exercises to strengthen the muscles. After the immobilization period is over, the strengthening program progresses from isometrics to using rubber tubing and then to dumbells or other weight exercises. Again, the strengthening program followed should be directed and supervised by a physician. Generally, sports medicine professionals allow an athlete to return to action when his or her internal and external rotation strength equals 20 percent of body weight.

Shoulder Subluxation

Subluxations are partial dislocations in which two articulating bones (bones that share a joint and are connected) separate partially.

Shoulder subluxation can be caused by one traumatic event, such as a dislocation, or by a movement that repeatedly places abnormal stress on the joint. The head of the humerus is more prone to subluxing (moving forward) when the supporting ligaments and tendons are repeatedly stretched. When subluxation occurs, the athlete feels as though his or her shoulder came out of its socket; then the athlete may have sudden pain along the arm and numbness in the fingers, which may last for several minutes. Then the arm feels weak. Often there is point tenderness on the front of the shoulder, and any external rotation is uncomfortable.

If one of your athletes has a subluxation, immobilize the shoulder with a sling or a shoulder immobilizer, apply an ice pack, and refer the athlete to a physician. Usually the shoulder is immobilized for several weeks, and then the athlete follows a gradual, intense program of strength and flexibility exercises, as prescribed by the physician. An athlete who has recurrent subluxations may not need to see the physician every time, but follow the protocol for dislocations—immobilization, icing, rest, and exercises. The athlete can return to play when the shoulder is free of pain throughout the full range of motion. Due to the nature of the sport, taping the shoulder for support and to restrict movement usually is not effective or comfortable for the athlete. Reconstructive shoulder surgery is often used to treat recurrent subluxations.

Elbow Contusions

The elbow lacks soft tissue padding and is vulnerable to bruises, or contusions. This is especially a problem for volleyball players, who dive to the floor often. A contusion may result from one good blow to the elbow or from repeated blows, and it can swell rapidly. Such injuries should be treated with ice 3 to 4 times and with compression with an elastic bandage for at least 24 hours. For a severe injury in which there is extreme pain and tenderness on the bone, refer the athlete to a physician to have the area x-rayed.

Repeated blows may also result in bursitis, an inflammation of the bursa. A bursa is a fluid-filled sac that lubricates areas of the body where friction occurs, such as where muscles and tendons cross bony prominences.

A bruised elbow should be protected from further blows until there is no more tenderness in the area. This can be done with padding. Use a 1/2-inch thick pad, cut it to fit the area, and secure it with tape or a wrap.

Wrist Sprain

A wrist sprain, the most common wrist injury, is usually incurred when the athlete falls on the wrist when it is hyperextended. Symptoms of a sprained wrist include pain, swelling, and the inability to flex and extend the wrist due to discomfort. A severe sprain is characterized by extreme pain on or near a bone or bone(s) and decreased range of motion due to pain. Also, the athlete may hear a crack or pop at impact. Refer athletes with severe wrist sprains to a physician.

Mild and moderate sprains should be treated with cold therapy and compression with an elastic bandage; ice should be applied for 20 minutes two to three times per day. The athlete may wear an elastic bandage wrap for support during the day, if that makes him or her feel more comfortable. The athlete can return to play when he or she regains full range of motion, but the wrist should be supported with tape (see Figure 5.9).

Once the acute pain has decreased, have the athlete work on wrist strength and range of motion. Figure 5.10 shows good exercises for this. The athlete flexes and extends the wrist with a closed fist, bends the wrist laterally back and forward, and rotates the palm up (supination) and down (pronation). When the athlete can do these motions without much pain, have him or her do them while holding a weight, beginning with a 1-pound weight and working up to 5 pounds. Have them do 2 to 3 sets of 10 to 15 repetitions. Squeezing a tennis or racquet ball is another way to improve wrist strength.

Finger Sprains, Fractures, and Dislocations

Volleyball players tend to incur finger sprains, fractures, and dislocations while blocking or setting. Blocking is commonly the cause for thumb injuries. The impact of the ball forces the thumb into hyperextension and abduction (movement away from the midline). When an athlete injures a finger or thumb, check for deformities that would indicate a fracture or dislocation. If there is deformity, and the athlete heard or felt a crack or pop on impact or experiences a loss of motion, splint the injured area and refer the athlete to a physician. If those signs are absent, test for range of motion. Note where the pain is, its severity, and whether there

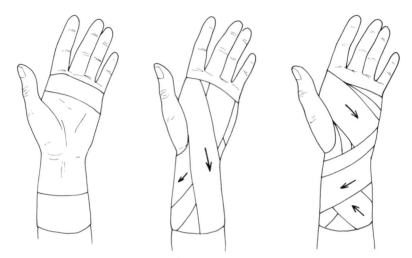

The rehabilitation of some wrist injuries requires limiting wrist flexion or extension. Following are the taping procedures offering *moderate support*.

1. Wrap several layers of underwrap around the palm and wrist in a figure-eight pattern. Apply one or two layers of underwrap at the wrist and then angle up across the back of the hand, between the thumb and index finger, and down across the palm. Repeat this process twice.
2. Place an anchor strip around the forearm, about 3 inches above the wrist (styloid processes).
3. Place a second anchor strip just below the knuckles, keeping the fingers spread during the process.
4. The wrist must be moved (flexed or extended) in the direction opposite that which causes discomfort and kept in this position until the procedure is completed.
5. Use strips of tape to form a crosscross pattern. To restrict flexion of the wrist, apply tape to the back of the hand; to restrict extension, apply tape to the palm. Begin the first strip at the anchor below the little finger, pull it across the wrist, and attach it to the forearm anchor. The second strip is applied to the anchor below the index finger. Pull it across the wrist and attach it to the forearm anchor. This crisscross pattern is repeated three more times.
6. Two figure-eight patterns of taping are applied over the top of the crisscross pattern.

Figure 5.9 Wrist support taping.
Note. From *Coaches Guide to Sport Injuries* (pp. 208, 209) by J.D. Bergeron and H.W. Greene, 1989, Champaign, IL: Human Kinetics. Copyright 1989 by J. David Bergeron and Holly Wilson Greene. Reprinted by permission.

Wrist flexion strengthening

While seated, lay your forearm on the table with the wrist over the edge and the palm facing the ceiling. Hold your forearm with your other hand while slowly raising the weight, moving your hand toward you, then slowly returning the hand to where you started.

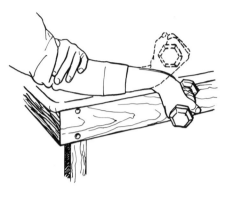

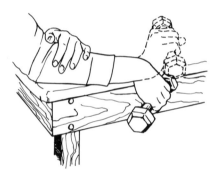

Wrist extension strengthening

Start in the same starting position as for the wrist flexion exercise *except* turn your palm face down. Stabilize the forearm with the other hand. Raise the weight up toward you as far as possible, then slowly return the hand to where you started.

Ulnar and radial deviation

Stand holding your arm at your side, with the *end* of a weight in your hand. Bend your wrist laterally back, then slowly return to where you started. Bend the wrist laterally forward. Be sure that the movement occurs only at the wrist.

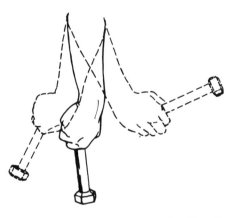

(*continued*)

Figure 5.10   Forearm- and wrist-strengthening exercises.

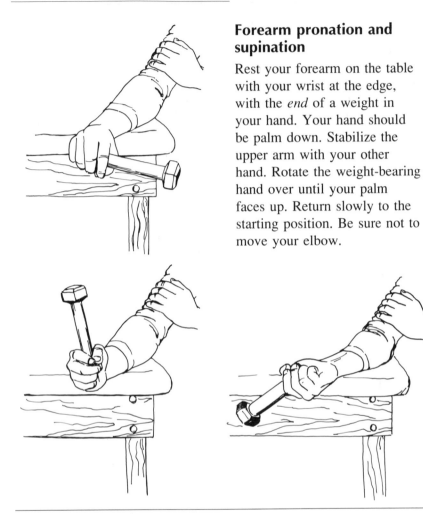

Forearm pronation and supination

Rest your forearm on the table with your wrist at the edge, with the *end* of a weight in your hand. Your hand should be palm down. Stabilize the upper arm with your other hand. Rotate the weight-bearing hand over until your palm faces up. Return slowly to the starting position. Be sure not to move your elbow.

Figure 5.10 *(continued)*

is swelling. Then immediately apply ice, elevate the injured area, and begin compression by wrapping the finger with tape, preferably stretch tape. Ice the finger by putting it in a cup of ice water.

If a finger joint is sprained, "buddy tape" the injured finger to an adjacent finger for support above and below the joint involved (see Figure 5.11). A thin piece of foam or felt can be placed in between the fingers for comfort. The injured area should be taped throughout the day for the first 2 to 3 days so it can rest. If the thumb is sprained, support and protect it from further injury by taping (see Figure 5.12).

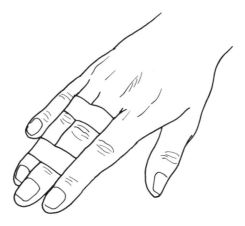

Figure 5.11   Buddy taping fingers.
Note. From *Coaches Guide to Sport Injuries* (p. 210) by J.D. Bergeron and H.W. Greene, 1989, Champaign, IL: Human Kinetics. Copyright 1989 by J. David Bergeron and Holly Wilson Greene. Reprinted by permission.

The finger or thumb should be iced three to four times per day, and the athlete should work on flexibility (range of motion). As soon as possible, the athlete should begin strengthening exercises. Squeezing a tennis ball is a good strengthening exercise. Another good one is to put rubber bands around the fingers and then open and close the fingers.

Practice time lost due to finger injuries should be minimal, if any. The athlete can practice the next day, being sure to buddy tape the finger.

Knee Injuries

The knee is the largest joint in the body, but it is extremely vulnerable to traumatic and overuse injuries. Acute knee injuries should be assessed quickly and thoroughly because they can be serious. Chronic injuries, such as tendinitis, are not as serious but you should be concerned about them as well. Any knee injury requires prompt attention, evaluation, treatment, and rehab to best ensure a full recovery.

Knee Tendinitis.   Sudden and repetitive jumping, which requires forceful extension of the knee, may begin an inflammatory process in the patellar tendon that can develop into chronic tendinitis. (The patellar tendon on the front of the leg connects the patella, or kneecap, to the tibia, or shinbone.) It is not uncommon for volleyball players to develop patellar tendinitis, a condition not easily cured.

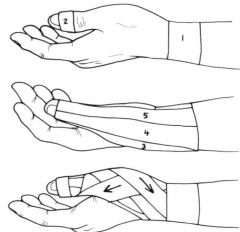

Most often, any therapeutic taping of the thumb is done as part of the rehabilitation of a minor thumb sprain. The materials needed include tape adherent and 1-inch athletic tape. The procedure requires you to do the following:

1. Apply tape adherent around the wrist and base of the thumb.
2. Place one anchor strip around the wrist. Keep this anchor loose.
3. Place another anchor at the distal end of the thumb.
4. Four strips of tape should be applied from anchor to anchor along the injured side of the thumb (back or palm side). These should be held in place with one strip of tape applied around the wrist and a second strip placed around the distal thumb.
5. Three additional strips of tape (spica) are added. When pain occurs with movement away from the midline (abduction), start the first strip at the base of the thumb on the palm side of the hand. Angle this strip upward under the thumb, encircle it, and bring the tape around to the back (dorsal side) of the hand. The tape should crisscross over the outside of the thumb to form an X. Fold over the edge of the tape as you apply it to the web space to reduce irritation. Continue the tape around the wrist and end at the starting point to form a figure eight. Place the second strip so that it will overlap the first one by two-thirds, and encircle the thumb at a more distal point. The third strip should be applied the same way, overlapping the second strip by two-thirds. Be careful not to encircle the thumb too tightly; circulation can easily be hindered.
6. Apply an anchor strip at the wrist to secure the tape ends.

This method of thumb taping will help protect the joints and muscles of the thumb, especially in cases involving pain during abduction (away from the midline). If the pain occurs on adduction (movement toward the midline), the same basic procedure is applied; however, the spicas are applied starting at the base of the thumb on the dorsal surface.

Figure 5.12 Thumb support taping.
Note. From *Coaches Guide to Sport Injuries* (pp. 210-211) by J.D. Bergeron and H.W. Greene, 1989, Champaign, IL: Human Kinetics. Copyright 1989 by J. David Bergeron and Holly Wilson Greene. Reprinted by permission.

Patellar tendinitis has three stages of pain. In Stage 1 the athlete usually experiences pain only after sports activity. In Stage 2, the athlete can perform at the appropriate level but has pain during and after activity. In Stage 3, the athlete has pain during activity and prolonged pain after activity. This pain hampers performance and may progress to constant pain throughout the day. It's best to recognize and treat this injury in Stage 1, before it progresses in severity.

Treatment for first- or second-stage tendinitis should begin with warming the tendons for 10 to 15 minutes. This can be done in a whirlpool at 100 °F to 102 °F or with a moist heat pack. The athlete should apply a gradual static stretch while the tendons return to normal temperature. If the athlete is going to practice, this can be followed by a gradual exercise warm-up. If necessary, modify the skills the injured athlete works on in practice, the intensity, and the duration. Always do ice therapy after exercise. Apply an ice bag for 20 minutes or use an ice cup for 10 minutes.

So the tendinitis doesn't get worse, an athlete should stop exercising if he or she has pain during exercise. An athlete with third-stage knee tendinitis should rest the knee until it is symptom-free.

Rehab for knee tendinitis consists mainly of strengthening the quadriceps muscles, but you need to avoid exercises that require extending the knee. Knee extensions put excessive pull on the patellar tendon. Isometric contractions of the quad muscles and straight leg raises are good exercises for strengthening the quad muscles. Isometric contractions should be done three to five times per day (6 to 8 seconds each contraction, 3 to 4 sets of 10). Straight leg raises should be done with weights (3 to 4 sets of 15 to 20). Use just enough weight to make the muscle tired by the last few repetitions of each set.

Osgood-Schlatter Disease. Osgood-Schlatter disease develops in the immature adolescent knee. It typically affects athletes between the ages of 9 and 13, the period of most rapid growth. It is caused by repeated avulsion (tearing away of tissue) and inflammation of the patellar tendon at the epiphysis (growth plate) of the tibial tuberosity. The chief symptom is severe pain on kneeling, knee extension, running, and jumping. Also, there is point tenderness over the tibial tuberosity, and the front of the knee may appear enlarged.

If an athlete has any of these symptoms, refer him or her to a physician. Treatment for Osgood-Schlatter disease is usually conservative and focuses on the symptoms. For example, the athlete is told to decrease or restrict stressful pain-causing activities until the pain subsides. And usually the pain does go away, as the epiphysis closes, which can take 6 months to a year. Other treatments include ice therapy before and after activity, isometric strengthening of the quadriceps and hamstring muscles, and extra padding in the knee pads to avoid bruising the prominent tibial tubercle.

Acute Knee Injuries.   With all the quick lateral and explosive movements volleyball players make, acute knee injuries are not uncommon. Knee injuries can be severe, so any athlete with a knee injury should be referred to a sports medicine professional. As the first person to learn of the injury, the coach is responsible for making the initial evaluation (e.g., determining whether to call an ambulance, to use a splint or crutches, etc.) and providing immediate care.

The key to understanding the knee injury is to know how it occurred. If you did not see the injury occur, ask the athlete to describe what happened. This information is pertinent to understanding the injury and what structures may be involved. If the athlete felt or heard a pop or snap and felt the knee shift, there may be ligamentous and/or meniscal tearing.

Immediately after any knee injury, apply an ice bag for 20 minutes, elevate the injured knee, and use an elastic bandage wrap for compression and support. (Wrap the bandage upward from midcalf to midknee to help minimize swelling.) The player should use crutches if standing or walking is uncomfortable and painful.

The sports medicine professional will prescribe a rehabilitation program that is appropriate for the severity of the knee injury. Generally, such programs include exercises to regain full range of motion, gradual strengthening exercises (starting with straight leg raises and progressing to using weights through the range of motion to increase quad and hamstring strength), and cardiovascular conditioning.

Muscle Strains of Quadriceps, Hamstrings, and Groin

A strain, or muscle pull, is a stretch, tear, or rip in the muscle or in adjacent tissue such as tendons. Most often a strain is produced when a muscle contracts abnormally due to fatigue, strength imbalance, or improper warm-up. Strains are classified according to severity (first-, second-, or third-degree strains) of tearing of the muscle fibers. Signs and symptoms that a strain may have occurred include a snapping sound when the muscle pulls, sharp pain during movement, muscle spasm, and extreme tenderness on touch. If you feel a ridge or an indentation when you touch the muscle, refer the injured player to a sports medicine professional. If you just find tightness, or a "knot," treat the injured area with an ice massage and wrap it with an elastic bandage. Reapply ice three to four times per day. Keep the injured area wrapped and rest it for at least 48 to 72 hours. The player may use crutches if walking is painful.

The injured player may do gentle stretching but only within pain limits. Do not let the athlete stretch ''through the pain.'' Once the acute inflammatory stage is over (after about 24 hours), the athlete may start isometric exercises. Instruct him or her to gradually stretch further, as the muscle heals, and then start using weights through the muscle's range of motion. Eventually the athlete will progress to biking and jogging. Once the athlete can complete all movements involving the strained muscle without pain, he or she can resume playing volleyball. But don't allow the return too soon, for muscle strains tend to recur—either because the muscle is not fully healed or because it healed with inelastic scar tissue.

Ankle Sprains

The sprain, common yet disabling, is a traumatic twist to the joint that stretches or tears the ligaments or other connective tissue. Sprains are graded in three degrees. First degree indicates stretching of ligaments, second degree indicates partial tearing, and complete rupture or tear describes the third degree.

Ankle sprains are generally due to a sudden lateral (ankle rolls inward) or medial (ankle rolls outward) twist. In volleyball this often happens when, after hitting or blocking, the player lands on a twisted ankle or on another player's foot, causing the ankle to twist. An *inversion sprain*, in which the foot turns inward, is most common due to the bony stability of the lateral side (the fibula is longer than the tibia, thus the ankle isn't able to evert as easily as it can invert). The result is damage to the lateral ankle ligaments.

Sometimes an ankle sprain is accompanied by a fracture of the tibia, fibula, or talus. (The tibia is the large, medial bone of the lower leg, the fibula is the smaller, lateral bone, and the talus is located at the end of these bones, in the ankle.)

When a player is injured, the coach should evaluate the severity of the injury. If the athlete has point tenderness directly on the bone, or felt something pop or crack, immobilize him or her, and arrange for the player to be seen immediately by a physician. Immobilize the ankle with some type of splint, such as a pillow, boards, or premade splints. If the athlete is unable to bear weight, make sure crutches are used. When examining the injury, look for swelling (although the amount of swelling does not indicate the severity of the injury), local temperature increase, pain on touch, inability to bear weight or walk, and loss of motion. Note if the athlete has sprained the ankle previously, for recurrent ankle sprains are common.

You should also test the athlete's range of motion by having him or her plantarflex (point toes), dorsiflex (toes up toward leg), invert (foot turned inward), and evert (foot turned outward). Then test strength with these same motions, but this time provide some resistance. Provide enough resistance with your hand so that the athlete has to work to move the ankle.

After evaluation employ ICE-R (ice, compression, elevation, and rest) intermittently for 48 to 72 hours (see Figure 5.13). You'll want to minimize swelling, which often increases in amount in the first 12 hours after a sprain. To apply compression use a horseshoe-shaped pad made of 1/4-inch to 1/2-inch felt or hard foam (see Figure 5.14). Use an elastic bandage wrap to hold the pad in place; wrap from the toes upward. The injured area should be elevated almost constantly. Crutches should be used if the athlete has any discomfort with walking. Using crutches puts less stress on the ankle and gives it a chance to rest. Ecchymosis, or bruising, may occur 2 to 3 days after injury.

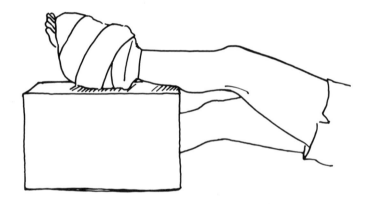

Figure 5.13   ICE-R for the ankle.

Figure 5.14   Ankle horseshoe.

After about 72 hours the athlete should begin taking contrast baths to help remove any remaining swelling. The contrast bath requires two buckets of water: one hot (100-102 °F), one cold (60-65 °F). The athlete alternately submerges the ankle in each bucket for about 3 minutes for five to six times, beginning and ending with cold water.

The athlete should begin range of motion exercises within 48 hours of the injury. Have him or her trace the alphabet with the ankle and foot; the movement should be at the ankle joint and not at the toes. The athlete should progress to strengthening the ankle joint by doing exercises with rubber tubing or applying resistance in the four motions discussed earlier (see Figure 5.3). Toe raises are also good for strengthening the ankle. Once weight bearing is pain-free, the athlete can start easy jogging with the ankle taped for support.

The athlete is ready to return to practice with the ankle taped when he or she can run figure eights and zig-zags, run backwards, and jump up and down without any pain. The injured player should continue to work on ankle strength even after resuming full activity. Ice therapy should be done after activity to reduce the chance for swelling. Apply an ice bag for 20 minutes. Sprains greater than a first degree tend to recur because of increased ligamentous laxity. This is why the ankle should be protected with tape or an ankle brace and strengthening exercises continued (see Figure 5.3).

PUTTING SPORTS MEDICINE TO WORK FOR YOU

The primary goals of sports medicine are to prevent injuries and illnesses and to treat those injuries and illnesses that do occur promptly and completely so that sidelined athletes can return to action quickly.

Injury prevention can start with you. Teach and demonstrate the correct volleyball skills. Combining this with a carefully planned, year-round conditioning program will assist greatly in reducing your players' injuries. Injuries happen in all sports, so you must have a knowledge base on the evaluation, treatment, and rehabilitation of injuries. You also need to know when to refer an injured player to a physician. It is essential to also use resources in your community so that your athletes have the best chance for a speedy recovery.

Try to have an open mind about injuries so that athletes will freely come to you when they are injured. Athletes want to please the coach. Too often an injured athlete may not say anything and will try to play with an injury because he or she is unsure how the coach will respond. Keep an injured player involved with the team as much as possible. Also keep the team involved with the injured athlete. Explain the injury to the team—how it happened, how it could have been prevented, what's going to happen now, and when the athlete will be back.

By preventing and properly managing injuries, you give your volleyball players the chance to attain team and individual goals of success. This is the essence of sports medicine.

KEYS TO SUCCESS

- **Use the sports medicine professionals in your community.**
- **A team's success is inversely related to the number of injuries, so preventing injuries is a key to success.**
- **You, the coach, are responsible for teaching correct playing skills, which also helps to reduce the risk of injury.**
- **The most effective way to minimize acute and chronic injuries is through preventive measures such as conditioning, strength training, flexibility exercises, and proper nutrition.**
- **Always have the injured athlete participate in some type of exercise and have an active role with the team.**
- **For acute injuries use ice, compression, and elevation; for chronic injuries use heat before practice and ice after practice.**
- **The safety and well-being of the athlete should always have the highest priority.**

CHAPTER 6

Nutrition:
The Winning Diet

Gale Beliveau Carey
University of New Hampshire

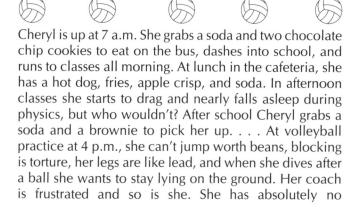

Cheryl is up at 7 a.m. She grabs a soda and two chocolate chip cookies to eat on the bus, dashes into school, and runs to classes all morning. At lunch in the cafeteria, she has a hot dog, fries, apple crisp, and soda. In afternoon classes she starts to drag and nearly falls asleep during physics, but who wouldn't? After school Cheryl grabs a soda and a brownie to pick her up. . . . At volleyball practice at 4 p.m., she can't jump worth beans, blocking is torture, her legs are like lead, and when she dives after a ball she wants to stay lying on the ground. Her coach is frustrated and so is she. She has absolutely no

131

energy . . . . At 6 p.m., it's straight to babysitting at the O'Donnells'. Nice of them to leave potato chips and dip to hold her over. . . . Home by 10 p.m.—too late to practice piano—she finishes French and calculus homework while eating leftover lasagna, then falls asleep at 11 studying physics. Why is she so tired?

Busy schedules, eating on the run, trying to fit it all in—this describes the lives of many athletes today. Why the lack of energy? Is it because of the busy schedule? Or is it because of poor nutrition? Let's change our athlete's diet and see what happens after a couple of weeks:

Cheryl is up at 6:45 a.m. She has a bowl of cereal, a banana, and two pieces of peanut butter toast and is out the door. She dashes into school and scampers to classes all morning. At lunch in the cafeteria, Cheryl eats spaghetti, bread, green beans, fruit cocktail, and milk. Physics class is still boring, but at least she stays awake. . . . At volleyball practice her legs feel great, she has lots of spring, she's really up in the air and crushing the ball. She still needs some work on her jump serve, though. . . . Cheryl goes straight to babysitting at the O'Donnells' after practice. She has a brown bag dinner—turkey sandwich, crackers, apple, milk, and cookies. The kids are wild, but they're in bed by 7:30. . . . Home by 9:30, Cheryl still can't practice piano, as little brother Kevin's asleep. She snacks on popcorn while reviewing physics notes for the test tomorrow. In bed by 11:15, she prays that the test isn't too hard.

Just as a change of diet made a big change in Cheryl's case, eating habits can make the difference between an above average player and a player that shines.

WHY NUTRITION IS IMPORTANT

For athletes, good nutrition is critical. Volleyball players put a lot of stress on their bodies, striving to jump higher and hit harder. The energy lost must be replenished, and the only way to do that is by eating properly.

To the body, food provides energy; it also provides structure. From infancy to adulthood, our bodies process food and convert it into either structure or energy. The body makes an eyelid or stores energy to blink that eyelid; it makes muscle, or it gathers energy to contract that muscle. Food is how we grow, and good nutrition is essential for building structure. You really are what you eat.

It's easy to see food turned into structure, such as bones, muscles, and hair, but food turned into energy isn't visible. Food energy comes from fats and carbohydrates. Food also provides vitamins and minerals, which help the body harness energy from fats and carbohydrates.

NUTRITIONAL CONCERNS IN VOLLEYBALL

Nutrition can work for your team. But players need to understand what good eating habits are before they can practice them. Your players may look to you for answers to these questions:

- How can I maintain a high energy level for practices and matches?
- How much should I weigh?
- How soon before a match should I eat?
- Should I take nutritional supplements?

This chapter addresses these concerns and gives you tips on how to be a nutritionally aware coach.

Keys to Good Nutrition

What is good nutrition? Some people think it means eating your vegetables, others think it means avoiding snacks, and still others think it means taking a vitamin pill daily.

Good nutrition means eating foods that provide the body with the right balance of vitamins, minerals, energy, and water that it needs, every day. It sounds simple enough, but many people's eating habits are way off the mark. They take in too much of some nutrients and too little of others.

The key components to good nutrition for athletes are carbohydrates, water, and variety and balance in the diet. Together they provide the energy and nutrients athletes need for peak performance.

Carbohydrates for High Energy

Carbohydrates are critical for volleyball players, because muscles burn carbohydrates to get energy. The harder a muscle works, the more carbohydrates it burns.

If the muscle runs out of carbohydrates, it still functions but only at half speed, because now it has only fat to burn. Hitting becomes harder; jumping half the distance takes twice the effort. Have you heard of marathon runners "hitting the wall" and having to stop and walk? Their muscles ran out of carbohydrates.

The carbohydrate stored in muscle is called *glycogen*. Figure 6.1 shows how important glycogen is to athletes. The figure shows that the more carbohydrate in the diet, the more glycogen is stored in the muscle and that the more glycogen in the muscle, the longer athletes can exercise before becoming exhausted. Simply stated, the more carbohydrates an athlete eats, the more endurance he or she has.

Muscle glycogen can be formed only by eating food carbohydrates. If the amount of carbohydrate in the diet is not high enough, muscle glycogen levels will drop.

Carbohydrates are one of three macronutrients in foods. The others are fat and protein. *Macro* means big; macronutrients are nutrients present in large amounts in food. Macronutrients are the body's source of energy.

Macronutrients in food = Fat + Carbohydrate + Protein = Energy

Micronutrients—vitamins and minerals—are needed in much smaller

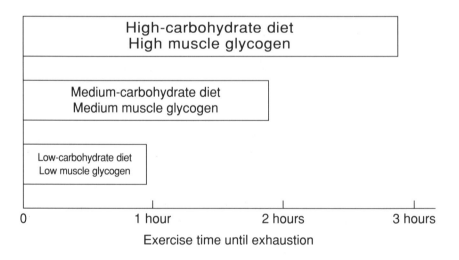

Figure 6.1   Effects of carbohydrates on muscle glycogen and endurance.
Note. From "Diet, Muscle Glycogen and Physical Performance" by J. Bergstrom, L. Hermansen, E. Hultman, and B. Saltin, 1967, *Acta Physiologica Scandinavica,* **71**, pp. 144-145. Adapted by permission.

quantities. But don't be fooled by the small amounts. Micronutrients are just as important. The vitamins and minerals provide no energy themselves but rather help the body extract energy from the macronutrients.

The body needs all three macronutrients because each serves a different function. Food protein provides the building blocks for body protein—muscles, hair, nails, digestive juices. Food fat provides energy for the body and chemicals essential for making hormones. And food carbohydrate keeps blood sugar levels normal and provides muscles with quick energy.

Food	**Body**
Protein ⟶	Muscles, hair, nails, digestive juices
Fat ⟶	Hormones, energy
Carbohydrate ⟶	Blood sugar, muscle carbohydrate, quick energy

The best diet for a volleyball player is one in which 60 percent of calories come from carbohydrate, 15 percent from protein, and 25 percent from fat. This chapter discusses how you can help athletes achieve this.

Because carbohydrates are a good energy source, you might think that players should eat plenty of carbohydrates the night before a big match or tournament. And this is true. But players also should eat plenty of carbohydrates at all times during the competitive season.

An experiment conducted several years ago demonstrated the importance of a high-carbohydrate diet. A group of healthy young men, ages 22 to 34, were asked to run for 2 hours every day and to eat a normal diet. Muscle glycogen levels were measured before and after the run each day. Then the men were switched to a high-carbohydrate diet, and the muscle glycogen measurements were repeated.

The results are shown in Figure 6.2. When the subjects ate the normal diet, they were gradually drained of muscle glycogen. In fact, by Day 3, several subjects were unable to complete the full 2-hour effort. On the other hand, when subjects ate the high-carbohydrate diet, they replenished their muscle glycogen stores each day, despite a heavy workout. They also felt that the run was a lot easier.

A high-carbohydrate diet is just as important for volleyball players. Daily practices of sprinting, jumping, blocking, and diving deplete muscle glycogen. The only way to replenish the glycogen is to eat carbohydrates. Later in the chapter I'll provide sample menus that show how easy this is to do.

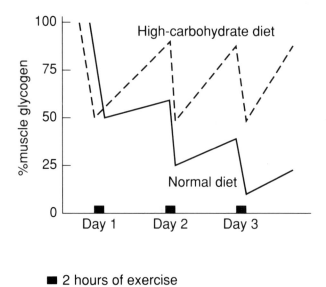

Figure 6.2 Effects of high-carbohydrate diet on muscle glycogen and exercise performance.

Note. From "Nutrition for Endurance Sport: Carbohydrate and Fluid Balance" by D.L. Costill and J.M. Miller, 1980, *International Journal of Sports Medicine*, **1**, p. 4. Adapted by permission.

How Much Protein?

It wasn't all that long ago that our thinking went like this: Muscle is made of protein. Athletes work their muscles very hard and must be breaking down those muscles. To build muscles back up, athletes should eat a lot of protein.

Now we know better. We understand that, yes, muscle is made of protein, but, no, it doesn't burn protein for energy. It burns carbohydrate and fat.

Although protein does not play the role we once thought, athletes still need protein in their diets. The young athlete who is still growing needs protein to form new muscle. In a full-sized athlete protein from the diet replaces the proteins that have been destroyed as part of normal aging. Protein also provides amino acids, which are needed to make certain hormones and regulatory factors so essential for normal growth, development, and performance.

How much protein should an athlete eat? For a growing teenager or young adult, the protein from 4 to 8 ounces of meat plus 3 to 4 glasses of milk each day is sufficient. For example, an athlete could eat cereal with milk for breakfast, a 2- to 4-ounce turkey sandwich with a glass of milk at lunch, milk with an afternoon snack, and a 1/4-pound hamburger and milk at dinner. Eating more protein than this doesn't cause the body to make more muscle. The only way to add muscle is through hard, physical work and good, balanced nutrition.

Getting Enough Water

A truly forgotten nutrient is water. About 60 percent of the human body is water. Water transports nutrients, oxygen, and carbon dioxide to and from the body tissues. It also lubricates joints. And most important, it maintains normal body temperature.

As the body's coolant, water has everything to do with performance. Intense exertion generates lots of heat, which must be gotten rid of. Water carries the heat away. Muscles generate heat, blood carries the heat to the skin's surface, and sweat releases this heat as vapor.

If the body keeps losing water, without a fresh supply of water coming in, it becomes overheated. Just like an overheated car, an overheated body will wear down and eventually stop.

The body loses a tremendous amount of water through sweat. A hardworking athlete can lose 8 pounds of water in 1 hour! Normally, sweat is released onto the skin's surface and evaporates into the air, carrying the heat with it. But on a humid day, the air is so full of moisture that the sweat cannot evaporate, and it rolls off the skin. The body is unable to cool itself properly on these days, and it also loses a lot of water.

In fact, when exercising in hot weather the body may need five to six times as much water as normal. If the body does not get enough water, dehydration occurs; the body's mechanism for cooling itself breaks down. As you know, this condition can be life-threatening.

To prevent dehydration, have athletes drink, drink, drink. Cool water is absorbed faster than water at room temperature, so have cool water (refrigerator temperature) available for your athletes, if possible. Impress upon your athletes the need to take in water all day long. Tell them to drink at least 8 cups of water a day. When the weather gets hot and humid, tell them to drink until they're visiting the bathroom frequently. Explain that they should never rely on thirst alone to tell them when to drink. By the time an athlete is thirsty, it is usually too late: He or she should have had water 30 minutes earlier.

What about electrolyte replacement drinks? These really aren't necessary. Players who eat a good, balanced diet replenish lost electrolytes through their diet. One glass of orange juice alone will replace all the electrolytes lost in 3 quarts of sweat. But many players like to drink these fancy drinks, and if so, let them. At least they are drinking. The most important thing is that they are getting water.

Striving for Variety and Balance

Another component to good nutrition is variety. There is no such thing as a perfect food—a food that has the proper balance of all essential nutrients, particularly the micronutrients. The names of all the essential vitamins and minerals are enough to boggle the mind. Pantothenic acid is bad enough. But molybdenum? Cobalamin? They sould like components of a nuclear bomb. How do we know where to find them, especially if we can't even pronounce them?

The best way to get the proper balance of essential vitamins and minerals, along with all the other essential nutrients, is to eat a variety of foods. The body can then pick and choose the nutrients it needs.

Variety means eating different foods from each of the six food groups: meat and meat alternatives, milk, grain and others, fruit, vegetable, and fat. Getting variety within the vegetable group, for example, doesn't mean eating cream-style corn one day, canned corn the next, and corn-on-the-cob the next. It means eating corn one day, broccoli the next, and carrots the next. Each of these vegetables has a different nutritional strength. Carrots are high in vitamin A, corn is high in carbohydrates, and broccoli is high in vitamin C.

Remember that carbohydrates are especially important for the athlete's diet. A diet rich in high-carbohydrate foods will provide high energy. Of the six food groups, three are sources of carbohydrates. The three are the grain and others, fruit, and vegetable groups. These should be emphasized in the athlete's diet.

In today's busy world, it is easy to get into a food rut, to eat the same foods day after day. Many people do this at breakfast, eating cereal, milk, OJ, and toast every day. By simply varying the kind of cereal, the kind of toast, and the topping for the toast and eating differently on weekends, you can break the rut and introduce variety. Although this can be challenging for young adults on the go, your making them aware of the importance of variety in the diet may help them change their habits.

A balanced diet has foods from each of the six food groups. Examples of foods from each of the food groups are given in Table 6.1.

Meat and Meat Alternatives.   Foods in this group are good sources of protein. This group includes animal products such as beef, chicken, turkey, eggs, fish, and lunch meats and nonanimal products such as beans, peanut butter, and tofu. The meat group provides an athlete with enough protein to keep the muscles healthy.

A little bit of meat goes a long way. People in the United States tend to eat much more meat than they need. Six ounces of meat per day should be plenty for an athlete. And some meats are high in fat, so knowing which meats are lean is a healthy advantage (see Table 6.1 for examples).

Milk.   The milk group is another good source of protein. It includes cheeses, yogurt, ice cream, and ice milk, in addition to skim or low-fat milk. Like some foods in the meat group, some milk foods are high in fat, especially ice cream and whole milk. Some people are lactose-intolerant; they can't digest milk products. These people have two alternatives: They can buy low-lactose milk products, which can be found on supermarket shelves, or they can make their own low-lactose milk by adding a special enzyme that is available in pill or liquid form. If these alternatives are not possible, the person should talk with a registered dietitian or family physician about taking calcium supplements.

Grain and Others.   High-carbohydrate foods are the cornerstone of a healthy diet. The grain group includes bread, cereals (hot and cold, except granola), spaghetti, noodles, pancakes, waffles, muffins, potatoes, and even corn (which is also a vegetable). These foods contain complex carbohydrates (also called starch): The molecules are connected like a strand of pearls. In contrast, simple carbohydrates (also called sugar) are molecules that are not attached to each other. Simple carbohydrates are found in table sugar, maple syrup, honey, and most cookies and candies. Athletes should concentrate on eating plenty of complex, rather than simple, carbohydrates.

Fruit.   Both types of carbohydrates are also found in fruits. Apples, oranges, bananas, pears, fruit juices, and fruit jam are good sources of carbohydrates as well as of fiber, vitamins, and minerals. But although fruit juices are part of this group, many contain very little fruit and are mostly corn syrup. Advise players to read the ingredient list on the juice container. The first item listed is present in the largest amount in the juice, the second item is present in the second largest amount, and so forth. If you want a real fruit juice, look for one with the fruit listed first or second on the ingredient list.

Vegetable.   Vegetables are another good source of carbohydrates, fiber, vitamins, and minerals. This group includes broccoli, carrots, celery, tomatoes, green beans, lettuce, and vegetable juices. Salad bars are a good spot to load up on vegetables, and raw vegetables are good snack foods.

Table 6.1

The Six Food Groups

Meat and meat alternatives

1 ounce lean beef, chicken, turkey
1 to 2 ounces fish
1/2 cup beans
10 medium shrimp
1 large egg

High-fat meats

1 ounce bologna, salami,
    liverwurst
2 strips bacon
1 ounce sausage
1 tablespoon peanut butter

Milk

1 cup skim or 2% milk
1 ounce mozzarella, Parmesan,
    or ricotta cheese
1 cup low-fat yogurt
1/4 cup low-fat cottage cheese

High-fat milks

1 ounce American, cheddar,
    or Swiss cheese
1 cup ice cream
1 cup hot chocolate

Grain and others

2 slices bread—wheat, white, rye,
    raisin
1 to 2 cups cereal
1 hamburger bun
1 cup oatmeal
3 medium pancakes
1 cup rice, spaghetti, noodles
1 cup corn
1 large baked potato
6 cups popcorn
2 large pretzels
1/2 cup sherbet
20 animal crackers
14 saltines

Fruit

1 apple, banana, grapefruit, orange,
    pear
3 tablespoons raisins
1/2 cantaloupe
40 grapes
1-1/2 cups strawberries
1/2 to 1 cup fruit juices
Jams and jellies

Vegetable

1 carrot, green pepper, tomato,
    cucumber
1 cup string beans, zucchini,
    mushrooms, corn
1 cup cauliflower, cabbage, rhubarb
1/2 cup broccoli, onions, squash, V-8
    juice
Unlimited lettuce

Fat

1 teaspoon butter, margarine, mayon-
    naise, oil
1 tablespoon cream cheese, heavy
    cream, sour cream
1 teaspoon Thousand Island, Roque-
    fort dressing
2 teaspoons French, Italian dressing
5 to 10 walnuts, peanuts, cashews,
    almonds
2 tablespoons sunflower seeds
1/8 wedge avocado

Fat.   The fat group includes nuts, seeds, salad dressing, butter, margarine, and alcohol. Fat also sneaks into foods in the meat and milk groups and into most prepackaged foods. People who eat lots of cheese, salad dressings, and regular cuts of meat eat a high-fat diet. High-fat diets are thought to increase the risk of heart disease, diabetes, and even some types of cancer. Being active doesn't make a person immune to these diseases. And eating a high-fat diet does not benefit an athlete's performance. The more calories athletes consume from fat, the fewer calories they will eat from carbohydrates, and the less quick energy they will have.

What About Vegetarians?   Some athletes are ovolactovegetarians: They avoid eating food obtained by slaughtering an animal but eat eggs, milk, and cheese. Some athletes are strict vegetarians: They eat no animal products whatsoever. Although all athletes should pay special attention to their diet, this is especially true for vegetarian athletes. Vegetarians may consume insufficient amounts of calories, iron, calcium, and vitamin B_{12}.

Because vegetarian diets tend to be low in fat but high in food volume, a vegetarian may feel full before he or she has eaten enough calories. If athletes are not sure that their caloric needs are being met, encourage them to visit a dietitian or sports nutritionist. Animal products are excellent sources of iron, calcium, and vitamin B_{12}, but these micronutrients are scarce in plant products. Strict vegetarians should take a vitamin B_{12} supplement, because this vitamin is found only in animal products. Good plant sources of iron include raisins, strawberries, broccoli, tomato juice, molasses, iron-enriched cereals, and iron-enriched breads. Calcium-rich plants include oranges, spinach, many types of greens, cornmeal, and molasses.

The notion that vegetarians must eat complementary protein sources—special combinations of plant foods at the same meal in order to consume the proper profile of amino acids—is based on experiments done on laboratory rats. Research done so far indicates this does not hold true for humans; experiments targeting athletes have yet to be performed. The bottom line? A vegetarian who eats sufficient calories and a balanced and varied diet should be consuming sufficient protein to meet amino acid needs.

The Supplement Story

Athletes want a competitive edge, and many athletes hope that supplements will provide it. Health food stores, drugstores, and even supermarkets have shelves loaded with vitamins, minerals, amino acids, lecithin, bee pollen, and sterols. Advertisements in muscle magazines promise greater strength to those who buy their special supplements.

More than 40 percent of high school and college athletes believe these ads and take supplements regularly, thinking supplements will improve their health and performance. Do supplements really help? No. Despite their popularity, supplements offer no proven benefit to an athlete who eats a balanced, nutritious diet.

One coach recently asked, "But aren't supplements good insurance, especially on days when you don't eat right?" Sure, taking a multi-vitamin-mineral pill will do no harm. For some, it may give a psychological boost. But vitamins and minerals don't provide energy by themselves; they only help to harness energy out of carbohydrates and fat. And taking megadoses of one or a few nutrients can be harmful, because certain nutrients are toxic in high levels (vitamins A and D, for example). Also, large doses of nutrients can upset the body's balance of other nutrients. Supplements are no substitute for Mother Nature, or good nutrition.

So what should you tell your athletes? Tell them that many scientific studies have tried to show a performance boost from supplements. But they have failed to show it. Unless an athlete is deficient in a nutrient, adding extra nutrients does absolutely nothing. Tell athletes that eating right is the best way to get the nutrients the body needs.

Now you know the keys to good nutrition, but what should volleyball players eat?

The Daily Diet

The ideal training diet for volleyball players is high in carbohydrate, low in fat, and moderate in protein. An athlete can attain such a diet by eating the right amounts from each of the food groups.

What to Aim For

Table 6.2 shows how many servings the average male and female volleyball player should eat daily from each of the six food groups. It assumes that the average male weighs 150 pounds and needs 3,200 calories daily and that the average female weighs 120 pounds and needs 2,400 calories.

How to Achieve It

How do these requirements translate into breakfast, lunch, and dinner? Table 6.3 shows sample menus that meet these food group needs for a typical male and female player. These menus provide plenty of carbohydrates, little fat, and adequate protein. And most importantly, these menus allow muscle glycogen levels to be kept high—which means plenty of muscle energy for high jumping and hard hitting!

Table 6.2

Food Group Servings for Volleyball Players*

	Meat	Milk	Fruit	Vegetables	Grain & others	Fat
Men	6	4	8	5	9	11
Women	4	3-4	6	4	7	7

*Note. This table assumes men weigh 150 lb and women weigh 120 lb.

In general, good nutrition can be achieved by eating from the six food groups and by getting balance and variety. But young male and female athletes may be missing specific nutrients.

Special Needs of Young Men

Male athletes may be low in three nutrients: folate, iron, and calcium. Folate is a B vitamin found in fruits and vegetables—two food groups that young, active people often skip. Many teenage boys are iron-deficient, especially athletic ones. And now that soft drinks have replaced milk at mealtime, young men are not getting enough calcium.

How can you advise your male players, so they won't be deficient in these nutrients? Tell them the following:

- Eat from the six food groups, especially fruits and vegetables.
- Eat red meats and iron-enriched cereals and breads.
- Drink milk at each meal and with a snack (4 cups per day).

Special Needs of Young Women

Teen and college-aged women tend to be low in the same three nutrients that men are low in: folate, iron, and calcium. Plus young women tend to be low in energy. Unfortunately, the deficiency of these nutrients has more impact on the health of females than of males. For example, later in life women have a tendency to develop osteoporosis, a condition in which bones weaken and break easily. The chances of this condition occurring are less if the woman consumed plenty of calcium when she was a young girl.

Once a girl begins menstruating, she loses extra iron each month. If enough iron isn't taken in, she can become anemic. A telltale sign of

Table 6.3

Sample Menus That Meet Food Group Requirements

			Men			
Meal	Meat	Milk	Fruit	Vegetable	Grain & others	Fat
Breakfast						
1-1/2 cups Cheerios					1	
1 cup 2% milk		1				1
1 large banana			1			
12-ounce glass orange juice			2			
2 slices toast with jam			1/2		1	
Lunch						
3 ounces tuna with	3					
1 teaspoon mayonnaise						1
on whole wheat bread					1	
1 cup coleslaw,				1		1
1 large sweet pickle				1		
12 potato chips						2
1 pear			1			
1 cup 2% milk		1				1
Snack						
2 cinnamon-raisin bagels					2	
2 cups lemonade			2			
Dinner						
3 ounces chicken breast	3					
2 cups rice					2	
2 cups steamed broccoli				1		
and carrots with vinegar				1		
Small salad with				1		
4 teaspoons Italian dressing						2
1 cup 2% milk		1				1
2 cups strawberries			1-1/2			
Snack						
6 fig bars					2	1
1 cup 2% milk		1				1
Totals	6	4	8	5	9	11

Table 6.3 *(continued)*

Sample Menus That Meet Food Group Requirements

			Women			
Meal	Meat	Milk	Fruit	Vegetable	Grain & others	Fat
Breakfast						
1-1/2 cups Cheerios					1	
1 cup skim milk		1				
1 large banana			1			
6-ounce glass orange juice			1			
2 slices toast with jam			1/2		1	
Lunch						
2 ounces tuna with	2					
1 teaspoon mayonnaise						1
on whole wheat bread					1	
1 cup coleslaw				1		1
1 pear			1			
1 cup 2% milk		1				1
Snack						
1 cinnamon-raisin bagel					1	
1 cup lemonade			1			
Dinner						
2 ounces chicken breast	2					
1 cup rice					1	
2 cups steamed broccoli				1		
and carrots with vinegar				1		
Small salad with				1		
2 teaspoons Italian dressing						1
1 cup 2% milk		1				1
2 cups strawberries			1-1/2			
Snack						
6 fig bars					2	1
1 cup 2% milk		1				1
Totals	4	4	6	4	7	7

anemia is shortness of breath and fatigue—this surely will affect her volleyball performance!

During the teens, body shapes change rapidly, and sometimes not to the liking of the body's owner. Some young women respond to these changes by dieting. But starving the body is not the solution. This approach weakens the body and robs it of essential nutrients and building blocks. It is much better to eat enough calories and burn them off with exercise than to eat too few calories and miss important nutrients. With time, the body's changes settle down.

What specific advice can you give to your female volleyball players about nutrition? Tell them the following:

- Eat from the six food groups, especially fruits and vegetables.
- Drink at least 3 cups of milk each day (4 for teenagers).
- Eat red meats, raisins, and iron-enriched breads and cereals. Have an annual checkup with a test for anemia to see if iron supplements are necessary. Better still is a serum ferritin test, which measures the body's stores of iron. A low serum ferritin level is a warning flag that anemia may develop and supplements should be taken.
- Don't skimp on calories! It's better to burn up extra calories exercising than to miss vital nutrients.

How Much Should Volleyball Players Weigh?

Because of all the jumping they do, volleyball players are acutely aware of body weight. They may not like the number, but they know what it is. And more often than not, they wish it were lower.

The Ideal Body Weight

What should players weigh to perform at their best? If they are too heavy, their jumping may falter. Too light and their hitting may weaken. Only a player can determine his or her best playing weight. There is no magical number that each player should weigh, but some general body weight guidelines for young adults, ages 18 to 25, are shown in Table 6.4.

Remember, these are general weight guidelines. In addition to sex and height, genetics play a big role in determining body weight. And so does the amount of muscle versus fat. For example, a 5' 6" woman who weighs 155 pounds is overweight by the standards in Table 6.4. But if her body is only 15 percent fat, far less than the average of 25 percent, then her weight is mostly muscle, not extra fat. The same holds true for men. The average body fat of American men is 15 percent, so an ''overweight''

Table 6.4

**Body Weight Guidelines for Volleyball Players
Ages 18 to 25**

Height		Men	Women
(ft)	**(in.)**	**(lb)**	**(lb)**
5	0		90–110
5	1		95–115
5	2	108–132	99–121
5	3	113–137	104–126
5	4	117–143	108–132
5	5	122–148	113–137
5	6	126–154	117–143
5	7	131–159	122–148
5	8	135–165	126–154
5	9	140–170	131–159
5	10	144–176	135–165
5	11	149–181	140–170
6	0	153–187	144–176
6	1	158–192	149–181
6	2	162–198	153–187
6	3	167–203	
6	4	171–209	

player with 8 percent fat needn't worry. Before advising players to lose weight, have their body fat measured by a trained exercise specialist. Your local sports medicine clinic should provide this service, but be sure a knowledgeable specialist does the measurement, as tiny errors in measurement can make big differences in the body fat percentage.

Ask your players, individually, about their health and weight. Not only will this show you're interested in them; you'll get information from them directly, rather than second- or thirdhand. If an athlete seems dissatisfied with his or her weight, ask why, and ask what his or her weight goal is.

When athletes want to change their weight, and their weight goals seem realistic to you, you can help by advising them with the following information.

Losing or Gaining Safely

It's natural for people to want immediate results, especially when it comes to changing body weight. Tell athletes that any weight change should be gradual to be effective. This goes for gaining as well as losing. Rapid weight loss is mostly water. Weight gained quickly may be mostly fat.

The athlete who wants to lose weight should primarily lose fat. And the one wanting to gain should add on mostly muscle. The following plan shows how an athlete can lose or gain weight while still getting proper nutrition from a balanced diet.

Have the athlete who wants to lose weight record how many servings he or she eats from the six food groups listed in Table 6.1 every day for 1 week. Give him or her a special notebook for the task to provide incentive. At the end of the week, have the athlete total the number of servings from each group and divide each total by seven. This gives the average daily number of servings. Next, subtract 5 servings of fat and 2 servings of grain from the average daily totals. This removes about 500 calories. Instruct the athlete to target the new totals each day, and encourage him or her to chart food servings daily. The athlete should lose about 1 pound a week.

For the athlete who wants to gain weight, the system is similar. He or she keeps a record and determines his or her average daily food-group servings. But then the athlete adds 1 meat, 2-1/2 grains, and 2 fats to the average daily totals. This adds 500 calories per day; again, about 1 pound per week.

It's important to approach your players about their weight and health. Listening to them will clue you in on issues that may severely affect health and performance. One of these issues, which unfortunately is common today, is eating disorders.

Watching for Eating Disorders

A person with an eating disorder has an intense preoccupation with food. His or her behavior may range from outright starvation (anorexia) to binge eating followed by vomiting, fasting, or using laxatives to get rid of unwanted calories (bulimia). Both anorexia and bulimia are prevalent in young adults today, especially college females. Eating disorders also affect men and are particularly high among athletes, male or female. It is thought that bulimia affects four times as many people as anorexia.

The cause of eating disorders is unclear. Our society constantly sends messages that "thin is in," especially for women, and this social pressure may be too overwhelming for people with certain personalities. People with eating disorders are often perfectionists and high achievers. They also see themselves as fat even when they are quite thin, and they are intensely afraid of becoming obese.

Eating disorders can be difficult to spot. How do you know if a player is anorectic? He or she is probably below the minimum weight for height listed in the guidelines in Table 6.4. He or she may convey to you (or to teammates) an intense fear of gaining weight. You may notice that a player exercises to exhaustion and, perhaps, fails to eat dinner when the bus stops after an away match. A person with anorexia may also lose hair and even show confused thinking. Females may miss menstrual cycles.

Bulimia is even harder to recognize. People with bulimia often appear physically healthy and are usually within a normal weight range. But emotionally they can be depressed and even suicidal. (By the time people with bulimia seek professional help, 5 percent of them have attempted suicide.) Weight swings of 10 pounds or more caused by binge-fast cycles may clue you in. Skipping postgame meals or making frequent trips to the restroom after meals could be tip-offs. Red knuckles, tooth decay, or a puffy face, especially around the eyes and below the cheeks, indicate vomiting episodes. Like people with anorexia, those with bulimia are overly concerned with body weight and shape.

An eating disorder may impair an athlete's performance by reducing his or her energy level. It also can cause serious medical problems. These include dizziness, electrolyte imbalance, menstrual problems, kidney failure, liver damage, and even heart failure.

The American Anorexia/Bulimia Association has an up-to-date listing of centers that offer therapy for eating disorders. The association's phone number and address are listed under "Resources" at the end of the chapter.

Avoiding Off-Season Weight Gain

Many athletes maintain weight during the competitive season but find the pounds beginning to sneak back on once the season ends. By the time the next season rolls around, they have quite an extra load to lug. The reason for this is simple: After the season ends, their eating continues, but their training does not. They consume more calories than they burn.

When you talk with athletes about weight and health, find out whether off-season weight gain is an issue with them. Female athletes are particularly prone to this problem. They needn't get down on themselves about it. We all get accustomed to eating a certain amount of food, and the shift from an active to a sedentary lifestyle won't change those habits overnight.

Offer the following tips for avoiding off-season weight gain to your athletes as your season closes down:

- It's normal to continue eating as much food after the season as during it. After all, you're used to it.

- Instead of changing your healthy eating habits, find an alternative exercise to help burn off the calories, such as jogging, biking, tennis. An aerobic exercise is best, but any exercise will do. Plus, it will help keep you in shape.
- If you don't continue exercising, you will have more free time on your hands. When people get bored, they eat. So keep busy.
- Eat slowly. This way, you'll be more aware of when you are full. And when you get full, stop eating.
- Cut down on portion sizes, but don't cut out foods. There's no need to deprive yourself of fun foods!

Eating on the Day of a Match

You've prepared your team, physically and mentally. You've practiced serves, passing, and plays. You've decided on the best starting rotation. You've educated your players about the best training diet. You've come this far—you certainly don't want to lose all that hard work.

What to Eat Before Competition

You could lose it all if your players don't eat right come match day. Some dos and don'ts for match-day eating are listed in Table 6.5.

Players should not eat a meal less than 3 hours before match time. When a player eats a big meal too close to game time, blood that should be supplying muscles with oxygen and nutrients is busy absorbing nutrients in the intestine. Consequently, the muscles suffer.

Some players are "sugar sensitive" and should avoid eating sugary foods during the hour before a match. Eating too many simple carbohydrates stimulates the fast release of insulin from the body. Insulin is the key that unlocks cell doors and allows the simple carbohydrates to get in. That sounds good. After all, muscle cells burn carbohydrates. But with a fast release of insulin, sugar rushes into cells, leaving little behind in the bloodstream. Low blood sugar results in light-headedness, weakness, and a slightly foggy mind—not good qualities for a volleyball player starting a match. To find out if a player is sugar sensitive, have him or her drink a soft drink 30 minutes before a practice, and then see if he or she experiences the symptoms of low blood sugar. Better to find out during practice than during a match.

Remember, too, that fats and proteins slow down digestion, so it's best to keep these to a minimum. This goes for pregame as well as

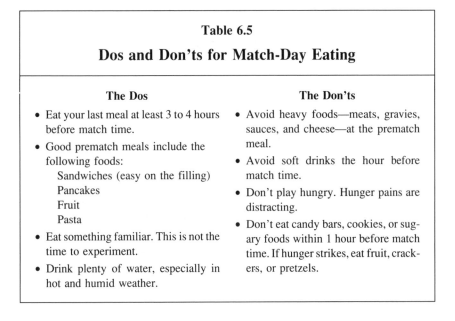

Table 6.5

Dos and Don'ts for Match-Day Eating

The Dos	The Don'ts
• Eat your last meal at least 3 to 4 hours before match time.	• Avoid heavy foods—meats, gravies, sauces, and cheese—at the prematch meal.
• Good prematch meals include the following foods: Sandwiches (easy on the filling) Pancakes Fruit Pasta	• Avoid soft drinks the hour before match time.
• Eat something familiar. This is not the time to experiment.	• Don't play hungry. Hunger pains are distracting.
• Drink plenty of water, especially in hot and humid weather.	• Don't eat candy bars, cookies, or sugary foods within 1 hour before match time. If hunger strikes, eat fruit, crackers, or pretzels.

between-match eating. The last section of this chapter has some suggested pregame meals.

What to Eat Between Matches

The dos and don'ts for pregame eating also apply to between-match eating. If the time between matches is 2 hours or less, advise players to stick to snack foods to prevent hunger. If the wait is 3 hours or more and is close to normal mealtime, then a high-carbohydrate meal may be in order. Eating between matches is not essential. Remember, most of the energy your players are using doesn't come from what they ate 1 or 2 hours before, but from what they've eaten over the past 1 or 2 days. But it is essential that players drink fluids, preferably water or sports drinks, between matches and that they avoid soft drinks. Sample suggestions for between-match eating are given at the end of the chapter.

What to Eat After Competition

After competition, your players should eat exactly what they should eat during training: a high-carbohydrate meal to replenish glycogen stores. Fast-food chains are the usual spot to stop after a match. Unfortunately, fast foods are generally high in fat and protein and low in carbohydrate. There are some exceptions, though, and the end of the chapter contains a healthy fast-food eating guide. Besides stopping at fast-food restaurants, think about suggesting a stop at a breakfast or pizza place. Pancakes, French toast, waffles, and pizza all make delicious high-carbohydrate meals.

PUTTING NUTRITION TO WORK FOR YOU

A major challenge for coaches is to put words into action. Diagramming a right side cross is one thing, but it takes getting onto the court and moving through the play again and again before it sticks. The same goes for knowledge on nutrition. You could tell athletes to read this chapter, but it is better for you to read it, then actively pass the information on to them. This section is designed to help you do just that.

Passing It On

You'll need to pass along some basic nutrition information to your athletes to lay the groundwork for healthy eating. One way to do this is to talk to them using some visual aids. Below are outlines for two short talks, 15 to 20 minutes each, that you can give before practice.

Talk #1

Your Goals
To explain where food energy comes from and how the body uses it
To show the importance of muscle glycogen to the athlete

You'll Need
A blackboard and chalk

Your Approach
1. Although you're not a nutrition expert, explain to your team that you do know nutrition is important. All hard work goes down the drain if proper foods aren't eaten.
2. Ask your athletes why they need food (answer: for energy and for maintaining and building their bodies). Ask them where the energy comes from (answer: fat, carbohydrate, and protein—not vitamins and minerals).
3. Outline the food sources of fat, carbohydrate, and protein. Explain that the body takes these and converts them into stores of fat,

carbohydrate, and protein. Explain that too much of any nutrient is converted into fat.

Your blackboard should look like this:

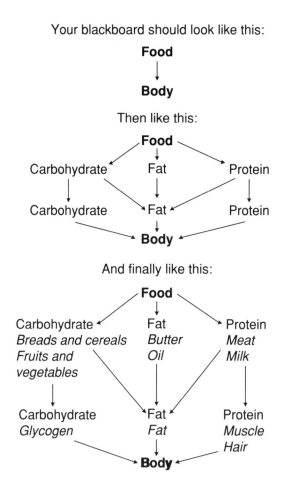

4. Explain that exercise uses fat and glycogen for energy but that glycogen is the key. The harder the exercise, the more glycogen is used up and must be replaced by food carbohydrates. If glycogen is not replaced, fatigue sets in. Draw the glycogen graph from page 136 on the blackboard.

Talk #2

Your Goals
To reinforce major points of Talk #1
To describe foods that are high in carbohydrate

To explain balanced eating from the six food groups

You'll Need

A blackboard and chalk

V-8 juice, a bottle of salad dressing, a carton of yogurt, a jar of peanut butter, a bagel, a Snickers bar, a doughnut

Your Approach

1. Review Talk #1. Ask your players where food energy comes from (answer: fat, carbohydrate, and protein). Ask what happens to it in the body (answer: fat is stored as fat, carbohydrate is stored as glycogen, protein builds muscle, hair, etc.; everything can be stored as fat if too much is taken in). Ask why athletes need plenty of carbohydrates (answer: to keep muscle glycogen stores filled— glycogen is essential for high energy).
2. Ask which foods have carbohydrates (answer: breads, cereals, bagels, spaghetti, macaroni, rice, potatoes, corn).
3. Ask about the rest of the diet. Introduce the idea of six food groups and write them on the board.
4. On the blackboard, write that a 150-pound man needs at least 9 servings of grain per day and a 120-pound woman needs at least 7 servings per day.

Your blackboard should look like this:

	Meat	Milk	Fruit	Vegetables	Grain & others	Fat
Men	6	4	8	5	9	11
Women	4	3-4	6	4	7	7

5. Players should also eat at least 6 to 8 fruits and 4 to 5 vegetables per day, 3 to 4 milk servings, and 4 to 6 ounces of meat per day.
6. Remind players that foods like doughnuts and candy bars have a lot of fat. This is OK, but suggest they try reaching for a bagel, a piece of fruit, or some toast and jelly instead (these are carbohydrates).
7. Ask players to guess which category the foods that you've brought with you belong to: V-8 juice (vegetable); salad dressing (fat); yogurt (milk and fat); peanut butter (meat and fat); bagel (carbohydrate); Snickers bar (meat, fat, carbohydrate); doughnut (carbohydrate and fat).

	Mon	Tues	Wed	Thurs	Fri	Sat	Sun	Goals
Table 6.6 **Nutrition Checklist**								
How many servings of *grain* did I have today?								7 to 9
How many servings of *milk* did I have today?								3 to 4
How many servings of *fruits* and *vegetables* did I have today?								minimum of 10
How many ounces of *meat* did I have today?								4 to 6
How many cups of water did I have today?								8

8. Tell them you can provide them with a nutrition checklist (see Table 6.6), and discuss guidelines for changing their body weight (see previous section).
9. Send them off, reminding them to eat their carbohydrates!

The Volleyball Players' Nutrition Checklist

A good way for a player to find out if his or her diet is up to par is by filling out a nutrition checklist. Give each player copies of Table 6.6 and of Table 6.1, which lists the six food groups. Encourage them to fill out the checklist each night for 1 week.

Sample Menus

Table 6.7 shows a week's worth of sample menus that provide a healthy diet of foods from the six food groups.

Table 6.7

Sample Menus for 1 Week

Breakfast	Lunch	Dinner	Snack
Monday			
Cereal, banana	Spaghetti and	Meat loaf	2% milk
2% milk	meatballs	Carrots and peas	Popcorn
Toast and jam	French bread	Potato and yogurt	Lemonade
Orange juice	Green beans	Salad	
	Fruit cocktail	2% milk	
	2% milk	Apple pie	
Tuesday			
Oatmeal with	Chili	Chicken breast	Cinnamon bagel
raisins	Rolls	Rice	2% milk
Toast and jam	Corn	Steamed broccoli	
Orange juice	Apple crisp	Whole wheat bread	
2% milk	2% milk	Strawberries	
		2% milk	
Wednesday			
Cereal, banana	Hamburger and	Pasta with vege-	Chocolate cake
2% milk	roll	tables and Parme-	2% milk
Toast and jam	French fries	san cheese	
Orange juice	Carrot-raisin	Whole wheat rolls	
	salad	2% milk	
	V-8 juice	Fruit bowl	
	2% milk		

Breakfast	Lunch	Fast-food dinner	Snack
Thursday (afternoon game)			
Cream of wheat	Tuna sandwich	2 hamburgers	Chocolate chip
Toast and jam	Tomato soup	Salad	cookies
Strawberries	Crackers	Vanilla shake	2% milk
Orange juice	Coleslaw		Popcorn
	2% milk		Lemonade
	Fruit gelatin		

Breakfast	Lunch	Dinner	Snack
Friday			
Blueberries, waffles, and syrup	Mexican salad	Shrimp and pasta	Melon and pineapple chunks
2% milk	Corn bread	Salad	Lemonade
Orange juice	Peaches	Whole wheat rolls	
	2% milk	2% milk	
	Sherbet	Strawberry pie	

Breakfast	Snacks between games	Fast-food dinner
Saturday (all-day tournament)		
Pancakes and syrup	Peanut butter on crackers	Pasta salad at salad bar
Orange juice	Oyster or graham crackers	Rolls
Muffins	Apples, oranges, bananas	Hamburger
	Rolls, bagels	Vanilla shake

Brunch	Dinner	Snack
Sunday		
Scrambled eggs, ham	V-8 juice	Popcorn
4 slices toast with jam	Roast beef	
Fruit cup	Potato Salad	
Orange juice and tomato juice	Peas and onions	
2% milk	Rolls	
	Angel food cake	
	2% milk	

Packing a Travel Cooler

A good one-time investment for your team is a cooler. You can take it on the road or use it at home to keep water and juices chilled (remember, cold water is absorbed faster than water at room temperature). Here are some other suggestions for cooler items, especially for away games:

- A jar of peanut butter and a knife
- 3 boxes of wheat crackers

- Fresh fruit
- Fruit juices in individual boxes
- 3 bags of pretzels
- Box of graham crackers
- Water

Eating on Match Day

Pregame meals, whatever time of day, should be satisfying but light. Two sample breakfast meals are

- cereal, 2% milk, whole wheat toast with jam, and orange juice, or
- pancakes with syrup, 2% milk, and orange juice.

Two sample lunch or supper meals are

- turkey sandwich, crackers, pickles, apple, and 2% milk, or
- spaghetti, bread, 2% milk, banana, and fruit gelatin.

Between matches, players should eat carbohydrates—bagels, crackers, apples, oranges, bananas, rolls—and drink plenty of water. Follow Table 6.8 guidelines for between-match eating.

After competition, restore glycogen stores with a high-carbohydrate meal such as spaghetti and meat sauce, thick-crust pizza, or pancakes with syrup.

Table 6.8
Between-Match Eating

Yes	No
Peanut butter on crackers	Soft drinks
Oranges, apples, bananas	Candy bars
Crackers	Sugary fruit juice
Dilute fruit juice	Deluxe hamburgers
Pretzels	French fries
Bagels	Potato chips
Water	

Fast-Food Eating Guide

Eating on the road can be tough on the budget, so most teams stop at fast-food chains. Eating nutritiously at fast-food restaurants can be a real challenge. Fast foods have a high-fat content, and such restaurants often do not offer fruits and vegetables. But salad bars, low-fat milk, and self-styled hamburgers have helped the nutritional standing of many fast-food chains.

Here is a list of some major fast food chains and suggestions for healthy food choices.

- McDonald's: hamburger or cheeseburger (not a Big Mac or super deluxe burger), salad, shake, sundae
- Wendy's: plain baked potato, chili, chicken breast fillet sandwich, single hamburger
- Pizza Hut: thick-crust pizza (go easy on the meat and cheese)
- Kentucky Fried Chicken: original recipe chicken breast, corn-on-the-cob, mashed potatoes
- Taco Bell: bean burrito, tostada, combination burrito
- Long John Silver's: coleslaw, ocean scallops, shrimp with batter, breaded oysters

Congratulations. You're ready to answer your volleyball players' questions on nutrition. Good luck and healthy eating!

KEYS TO SUCCESS

- **Your nutrition knowledge can make a big difference to your team's performance. Pass it on!**
- **Encourage your players to eat plenty of complex carbohydrates every day, not just the night before a match. A high-carbohydrate diet during the season means a high-energy performance. Muscle glycogen stores are used up by hard volleyball play, and they can be replenished only from food carbohydrates.**
- **Carbohydrates can be complex (starch) as in bread, pasta, rice, and beans or simple (sugar) as in candy, yogurt, fruit, soft drinks, and milk. Ask players to choose more complex carbohydrates than simple ones.**
- **Have players balance their diets by choosing from the six food groups: meat and meat alternatives, grain and others, milk, fruit, vegetable, and fat.**

- Encourage players to eat 3 meals a day plus snacks; discourage them from skipping meals. Their energy levels will be much more constant.
- If you are providing a pregame meal, serve it at least 3 hours before a match.
- Tell players to avoid simple carbohydrates the hour before a match.
- If hunger strikes before or between matches, offer players pretzels, crackers, or fruit to eat and water to drink.
- Be sure players drink plenty of cool water, especially on hot, humid days.

RESOURCES

American Anorexia/Bulimia Association
418 East 76th Street
New York, New York 10021
(212) 734-1114

American Dietetics Association
216 West Jackson Blvd., Suite 800
Chicago, IL 60606-6995
(800) 877-1600

> Extension-4852, Department of Nutrition Resources, for nutrition pamphlets and guidelines

> Extension-4841, Membership Department, for nutrition programs

> Extension-4893, Policy Administration, for state or local nutrition contacts

Anorexia Nervosa and Related Eating Disorders, Inc. (ANRED)
P.O. Box 5102
Eugene, OR 97405
(503) 344-1144

ACKNOWLEDGMENTS

Special thanks go to Jan Dainard, head coach of the women's volleyball team at the U.S. Naval Academy, Annapolis, MD, and George Carey, former assistant coach of the women's volleyball team at the U.S. Naval Academy and head coach of the boys' volleyball team at Oyster River High School, Durham, NH. Both provided me with valuable information, answered my questions, and allowed me time with their players to discuss nutrition issues.

Index

About the Editor

Carl McGown brings a broad range of technical knowledge and hands-on expertise to *Science of Coaching Volleyball*. His coaching experience spans more than 20 years and extends to all levels of the sport, including his work as Adjunct Assistant Coach for the 1984, 1988, and 1992 USA Olympic Men's Volleyball teams. He also has held various coaching positions for the USA National, USA Pan American, and USA World University Games teams. Carl is head coach of the men's volleyball team and a professor of physical education at Brigham Young University.

An avid volleyball player, Carl has been named All-American 7 times and has played on 11 National Championship teams in a playing career spanning 4 decades.

Carl earned his doctorate in motor learning from the University of Oregon in 1971. He has written many books and is a frequent contributor to such publications as the *Journal of Orthopaedic and Sports Physical Therapy, Research Quarterly for Exercise and Sport, Journal of Motor Behavior,* and *Journal of Teaching in Physical Education.*

About the Authors

Martin Gipson is a professor of psychology at the University of the Pacific. A long-time consultant to the USA Women's National Volleyball Team, he has worked closely with Terry Liskevych, PhD, the team's coach. He received a BA in psychology from California State University–Chico and a PhD in psychology from Vanderbilt University. Martin is a member of the Medical Commission of the Federation Internationale de Volley-Ball (FIVB) and has lectured and written on issues related to psychology and health psychology in sport and volleyball.

Steve Lowe died in August 1991. He was the head coach of women's volleyball at the University of Wisconsin–Madison and worked with Terry Liskevych as a consultant to the USA Women's National Volleyball Team. His academic background included a BA in psychology from the University of Iowa and an MA in psychology from the University of the Pacific. Steve served as the assistant coach of women's volleyball at the University of the Pacific under Terry Liskevych and present coach John Dunning; John and Steve's 1985 team won the NCAA

Division I National Championship. Steve's Wisconsin team won the National Invitational Volleyball Tournament in 1989 and the Big 10 championship in 1990. He was the coauthor of several articles on psychology and volleyball.

Thom McKenzie is a professor of physical education at San Diego State University. He has been a high school and club volleyball coach in Canada and is currently coinvestigator on two multimillion-dollar National Institutes of Health grants: Child and Adolescent Trial of Cardiovascular Health; and Sport, Play, and Active Recreation for Children. He is a long-time associate of Terry Liskevych and has consulted with the USA Women's National Volleyball Team for many years. Thom received a BPE in physical education and a BEd in education from the Uni-

versity of New Brunswick, an MSc in sport psychology from Dalhousie University in Nova Scotia, and a PhD in sport pedagogy and applied behavior analysis from The Ohio State University. Thom has authored numerous articles on sport and physical education.

Jim Coleman directs the National Volleyball Teams Training Center in San Diego, California. He has been associated with the USA National Teams since 1965, working as a head coach, an assistant coach, and an advisor for the men's team. Jim has been part of the U.S. Volleyball Association (USVBA) delegation at five Olympic Games, six Pan-American Games, four world championships, and seven North American championships. He began his academic career by earning an undergraduate degree in chemistry and physics from Wittenberg University. He

then did graduate work at the University of Kansas. While teaching at George Williams College, Jim became interested in physical education. After 20 years of teaching college chemistry, he pursued a master's degree in physical education at George Williams and a doctorate in education at Brigham Young University, where he studied under Carl McGown. Jim has been an active researcher and writer, and he is the U.S.A. representative to the North American Volleyball Federation and is on the International Volleyball Federation Rules of the Game Commission. In 1992 he received the honor of being inducted into the Volleyball Hall of Fame. Jim is the father of Kim ColemaNesset.

Kim ColemaNesset was a charter member of the Sports Performance Volleyball Program of Chicago's western suburbs when she was in high school. In the program she studied volleyball and physical training under Bob Gajda and Rick Butler. Kim continued her high school volleyball career in Walla Walla and Yakima in Washington, then played for Mick Haley at the University of Texas at Austin. She graduated from Texas with degrees in physical education and biochemistry and completed her master's degree in biomechanics at the University of California, Davis, under Keith Williams, in 1993. Kim married Jan Nesset in 1992.

G. Thomas Tait is an associate professor of exercise and sport science at The Pennsylvania State University (University Park campus), where he teaches exercise physiology, oversees the undergraduate program, and coordinates both the exercise science option and the senior internship program. He also teaches various levels of coaches' courses for both the Federation Internationale de Volley-Ball (FIVB) and the U.S. Volleyball Association (USVBA). He received a BS from the University of Maryland and an MS and a PhD from Penn State. As

an undergraduate, Tom was an Atlantic Coast Conference (ACC) and Intercollegiate Association of Amateur Athletes of America (IC4A) high jump champion and an NCAA medalist. He coached track and field at both the high school and collegiate levels for 8 years. After becoming involved in volleyball, he founded and coached the Penn State women's team for 4 years and coached the men's team for 15 years. Dr. Tait was named National Coach-of-the-Year in 1986 and was honored as Eastern Coach-of-the-Year a record five times. Between 1978 and 1988, Tait served as U.S. World University Games coach, U.S. Pan-American Games assistant coach, U.S. World Junior Championships assistant coach, and U.S. Olympic Festival head coach three times.

Jan Ochsenwald, who is both a registered nurse and a certified athletic trainer, is currently with Competitive Edge Health Services in Milwaukee, Wisconsin. There she is involved with the treatment of the general population, outreach programs at area high schools, and muscular biofeedback and reeducation therapy. Jan received a BS in nursing from the University of Minnesota, where she was concurrently in the Athletic Training Program, and an MS in sports medicine from the University of Illinois at Urbana-Champaign. Jan was at the Uni-

versity of Illinois for 10 years, first as a graduate assistant, then as a full-time assistant athletic trainer; her main responsibilities were with women's volleyball and men's and women's gymnastics. She was involved with many championship teams at conference and national levels. Her extensive experience with collegiate athletes has given her insight into helping athletes deal with the physical and mental aspects of injury and illness. While at the University of Illinois, Jan was a guest lecturer in the Department of Kinesiology and also presented various sports medicine topics to community groups. She has been a member of the National Athletic Trainers Association for 15 years.

Gale Beliveau Carey is an assistant professor in the Department of Animal and Nutritional Sciences at the University of New Hampshire. Her research focuses on intermediary metabolism, including amino acid and nitrogen metabolism in the liver and the regulation of fat mobilization from adipose tissue in response to exercise training. She has also studied the relationship between nutrition and performance in members of the University of New Hampshire swim and crew teams. Gale received a BS in biochemistry from the University of Massachusetts at  Amherst, an MS in nutritional sciences from the University of Wisconsin–Madison, and a PhD in nutrition from the University of California–Davis. She is a member of the American Institute of Nutrition, the North American Association for the Study of Obesity, the American Dietetics Association, and the American College of Sports Medicine. Gale opted for a career in science by default, when she realized at age 13 that she would never play first base for the Boston Red Sox. Her interest in sports continues: She enjoys long-distance running and road racing, and her baseball loyalties are split between Fenway Park and Oriole Park at Camden Yards.